THE COMPASSIONATE NOTARY

*A Field Guide to Notarizing
in Hospitals, Hospice and
the Homebound Signer*

Laura J Biewer

ISBN: 978-1-965971-30-7

> *"What you do makes a difference, and you have to decide what kind of difference you want to make."*
>
> JANE GOODALL

IMPORTANT LEGAL NOTICE

This book assumes you have already obtained your notary public commission for your state. Please be aware that the author is not an attorney, and the information provided in this book does not and is not intended to constitute legal advice. For legal questions or concerns, please consult with a qualified attorney in your jurisdiction.

With any business endeavor, your personal results will depend on your unique background, experience, capacity, and skills. Your dedication, desire, and motivation will also significantly influence the level of success you achieve.

Your use of any information, products, and services presented in this book should be based on your own due diligence. The author and the owners of any products and services mentioned are not liable for any success or failure of your business that is directly or indirectly related to the purchase and use of the information, products, and services reviewed or listed in this book or on related websites.

This book provides general guidance for facility bedside notarization. Notary laws vary by state and change over time. Readers are responsible for knowing and following their own state's current notary statutes, regulations, and administrative rules. When in doubt, consult your state's notary authority, the National Notary Association hotline, or a qualified attorney."

ADVANCED PRAISE FOR THE COMPASSIONATE NOTARY

Be that beacon of love and light when the public you serve needs it the most

As a mobile notary, you'll meet people on their best days...and their worst. Many of those appointments will take place in medical facilities, under extenuating circumstances that demand not only competence and professionalism, but compassion, and empathy. This book by Laura Biewer takes you by the hand and shows you the path to competence, confidence, and compassion. So, you in turn, can be that beacon of love and light when the public you serve needs it the most. There's a reason we all call Laura the G.O.A.T. Take this book to heart, and you will too.

BILL SOROKA
7-time Best Selling Author and Founder of *Notary Coach*

The insights and practical tips Laura shares here will prepare you for the most delicate signings with professionalism and heart

When I first heard that my mentor, **Laura Biewer**, was writing *The Compassionate Notary: A Field Guide to Signings in Hospitals, Hospice, and the Homebound*, my first thought was: *It's about time!*

Laura touched on much of this territory in *Beyond Loan Signings. Still, this* new work brings the often-overlooked area of general notary work—my own specialty as well—into sharper focus with the compassion and context it truly deserves.

These signings require a special touch: patience, empathy, and a solid understanding of the vast gray areas that often arise in medical and sensitive environments. In true Laura fashion, she provides not just theory, but clear, actionable guidance to help notaries succeed in every situation they might encounter.

For any notary ready to go beyond loan packages and basic documents, this book is indispensable. The insights and practical tips Laura shares here will prepare you for the most delicate signings with professionalism and heart. These assignments aren't for everyone, only a small percentage of notaries ever master the intricacies of working in hospitals, care facilities, and private homes—but thanks to this book, many more will now have a genuine opportunity to rise to that level.

It cannot be too highly recommended.

DANIEL BREWER; Beaverton, Oregon
Author of *The Book of Customer Service* (2025); Brewer Mobile
Notary Services; Founder, Notary Masters Speakers Bureau

I guarantee you'll return to the scripts and guides in this book time and time again

Right from the start, this book is packed with incredibly useful information. Notarizing in bedside environments is inherently challenging, but Laura Biewer guides you through nearly every scenario you might encounter with clarity and compassion.

She doesn't just offer advice, she equips you with tools, and lots of them. Two of my favorite chapters are:

- **Chapter 4: Intake and Prescreening** – A game-changer for setting expectations and ensuring you're prepared.
- **Chapter 10: Orienting the Signer** – This chapter emphasizes that assessment is key—ensuring the signer is both willing and alert.

What I appreciate most is how user-friendly this book is. The summaries and key takeaways at the end of each chapter are a resource in themselves. I guarantee you'll return to the scripts and guides in this book time and time again.

Honestly, I didn't know how much I needed this until I read it. *Great job, Laura.*

JOYCE M. GONZALEZ; Tracy, California
Owner, Convenient LiveScan And Notary (CLSAN.com)

I was blown away….my favorite is the intake form, I will be adding immediately

I was blown away at the level of detail that your book provides to notaries. As I read the book, I was thinking about all the things I should be implementing as I do bedside notarizations. One of the things that has been a recurring theme in my notary career is the use of intake form. I really appreciate you including this aspect in your book because it was so thorough and allows a notary to get the complete picture of the situation before the appointment. The intake form also allows a notary to look and sound more professional to the public as the questions are asked. No critical information can be missed when using an intake form on a regular basis. I really appreciate the time that you spent outlining all the various aspects of hospital / assisted living work. Each time you share your knowledge with the community we all become better and more proficient in our craft as notaries.

JEFFREY CLARK; Antioch, California
ACME LIVE SCAN and NOTARY

This is more than a guide; it is a lifeline

The Compassionate Notary is more than a guide; it is a lifeline for professionals called to serve at life's most delicate moments. Laura Biewer brings clarity, empathy, and experience to a part of our work that few are prepared for, but many will encounter. Her detailed frameworks, intake questions, and real-world examples give notaries the confidence to approach hospital and hospice assignments with both legal precision and human compassion. This book reflects the heart of our profession: protecting the public while honoring the people behind the signatures.

NICOLA JACKSON, aka Notary Nicola; Los Angeles, California

Laura has created more than a book, she has created a valuable tool for your Notary Bag

In hospitals, hospices, and the homes of the homebound, notaries face unique challenges and high-stakes, high-stress moments. The Compassionate Notary is the guide you can rely on to navigate these situations with confidence, and compassion. Laura has created more than a book, she has created a valuable tool for your Notary Bag, an essential resource filled with decades of real-world experience, practical tips, and strategies you can turn to again and again. This guide covers so much: intake and pre-screening, safety protocols, signer assessments, and navigating challenges or interruptions. It shows notaries how to protect themselves, set fair and appropriate pricing, and build a bedside notary brand the community trusts. It is packed with quick-reference tools, checklists, sample forms, and red-flag guidance. This book is more than a one-time read—it's a resource you can reach for in the moment, helping every bedside appointment run smoothly, and professionally. With this book in hand, you show up ready to serve, ready to make a difference, and ready to leave a lasting impact on families and clients.

SUSAN M. HOPE; California
Notary Public & Owner, *NotaryAssist Software*

For notaries who want to expand beyond routine notary work, this book is not optional, it is foundational

The Compassionate Notary is more than a book, it is a long-overdue elevation of what bedside notarization really represents in our profession: a fusion of legal duty, human sensitivity, and operational excellence. Laura has taken a niche, most notaries enter hesitantly and turned it into a highly teachable specialty grounded in clarity, structure, and respect for the people we serve. This book does what no state handbook, no loan signing course, and no Facebook thread has ever done: it walks the working notary, step by step, through the *full process* of a facility-based notarization. From intake scripting, to prescreening, to navigating the medical ecosystem, to capacity assessment, to documentation and post-appointment follow-through, this guide creates a standard of care that the profession needs. The book's greatest strength, however, is its balance; it never romanticizes bedside work, and it never catastrophizes it. Instead, it equips notaries with repeatable systems, tools, language, and decision frameworks that eliminate guesswork and lower the failure rate of facility signings, something notaries often struggle with in their practice. For notaries who want to expand beyond routine notary work, this book is not optional, it is foundational. It sets the benchmark for bedside notarization, and raises the bar for what ethical, prepared, and emotionally intelligent notary service looks like in everyday practice.

MATT MILLER
President, The California League of Independent Notaries

FIND FREE RESOURCES ON THE WEBSITE!

SCAN

https://www.coachmelaura.com/compassion-
ate-notary-resource-library-sign-up

TABLE OF CONTENTS

PREFACE

In 2001, I had the opportunity to own my first business, a six-bed residential elder care facility. I didn't know much about running this kind of business. I had no formal experience caring for seniors, and I didn't have the money for a down payment on the home. But the universe stepped in. Sarah, the woman retiring from the facility, believed in me. She offered to carry a second mortgage to serve as the down payment, making it possible for me to buy the business. She even stayed on for the first month, allowing me to learn the routine under her license while I completed the necessary training and passed the state exam.

Around that same time, I had a friend, Joyce Gandelman, an attorney who had put herself through law school by working as a notary. She performed notarizations at hospitals, skilled nursing facilities, and assisted living centers, and also handled loan signings. I told her how hard it was to get a notary to come to my facility—and how often I'd hear excuses: the patients were too slow, didn't have proper ID, or struggled to sign their name. Joyce encouraged me to become a notary myself. She knew the need was there and that she wouldn't be able to meet it much longer as her legal career advanced.

Joyce helped me get started with hospital work, which I did for free, and loan signings, for which I charged, so I could earn extra income, especially helpful when all six beds weren't full. She taught me how to communicate effectively with clients, assess their awareness, identify resources to tap into, and navigate family dynamics, while also offering practical tips for notarizing in medical environments. I discovered I loved notary work to the point that by my fourth year of owning a facility, I sold it and became a full-time notary.

WHY THIS BOOK MATTERS TO YOU.

Whether you're already performing hospital and bedside notarizations or just beginning to consider this path, the truth is that these calls will come, and the need may be urgent. And when they do, the stakes will be high. Families are relying on you to be both professional and compassionate, often during the most difficult day of their lives.

Not every notary feels confident walking into a hospital room. But those who do stand out. You don't just complete an appointment; you provide reassurance, clarity, and calmness. This work isn't for everyone, but for those willing to develop the right mindset and approach, the work of a bedside notary becomes one of the most rewarding niches in the notary profession.

That's why this book exists. To help *you* meet these moments with readiness and heart.

When someone calls a notary to a hospital or skilled nursing facility, it's rarely just business—it's personal. The documents may be urgent, the timing unpredictable, and the emotions intense. In these moments, notaries are not just witnessing signatures. They are witnessing life transitions.

This book is for notaries who want to be ready, not just technically, but mentally and emotionally, for bedside notarizations. These appointments require more than a journal and a stamp. They need kindness, flexibility, preparation, patience, and a profound understanding of the distinct dynamics within medical settings.

Inside, you'll find tips and insights drawn from over two decades of real-world experience. Each chapter focuses on a critical stage of the process, from intake to execution, with attention to the details that make all the difference. Whether you're just beginning to explore this niche or looking to refine your approach, this guide will help you serve with confidence and care.

Because when you show up prepared and fully **PRESENT**, you become more than a notary; you become a trusted presence during someone's most vulnerable moments.

Always at your Service,
Laura Biewer

FOREWORD

Author of *On The Move: The Relationship-Driven 5 Point Marketing System for Mobile Business Success*

The first time I met Laura Biewer, I knew two things: one, I was in the presence of someone with a mind like a steel trap; and two, she had a heart big enough to carry a whole community. Now, I call her my "notary bestie," but the truth is she's become one of my dearest friends, fiercest champions, and the notary world's equivalent of a lighthouse: steady, strong, and always guiding others through the storm.

So, when Laura told me she was writing a book about hospital notarizations, I didn't just say "Yes, please," but said, "Finally." No one is more qualified or compassionate to teach this incredibly important and often misunderstood niche of notary work.

This is not a book filled with generic checklists or dry theory. It's a masterclass in showing up fully, professionally, and with deep humanity, at someone's most vulnerable moment. Whether you're navigating an ICU hallway or a family's quiet heartbreak, Laura doesn't just prepare you for the logistics; she prepares your heart.

She walked through these halls, asked the tough questions, made the hard calls, and done it all with integrity that never wavers. Every page is soaked in lived experience and love for this profession and the people we serve.

If you are a notary who wants to do more than just "get the job done," if you want to *make a difference*, then this book is your map. It's also a reminder that our work is sacred, especially at the bedside.

Laura, thank you for your tireless leadership, your endless grace, and your unwavering friendship. The world, and the notary industry, is better because you're in it. And now, thanks to this book, countless notaries will be too.

With deep respect and even deeper affection,

Jen Neitzel

HOW TO USE THIS GUIDE

Whether you're brand new to bedside notary work or looking to strengthen your current practice, this guide was built to support you with real-world advice, flexible scripts, and step-by-step strategies. If you have taken training, have asked questions on Facebook, or watched youtube, you leave that behind when you enter the hospital. Having a resource that is easy to read, locate information you need, and is straight to the point is the kind of help that can make it look like you know what to do , even if you forgot. Dog ear, highlight, underline and circle the things you may need in this setting, know that you can trust yourself and your decisions when you have prepared.

Start where you are. If you've never set foot in a hospital as a notary, begin at Chapter 1 and read through in order, as each chapter builds on the one before it. If you already have some experience, feel free to skip around and zero in on what you need most right now.

Make it personal. Use the intake form and checklists to build your own bedside appointment process. Tweak the suggested scripts to reflect your tone. Add notes to the glossary to reflect how your state handles procedures for credible witnesses or signatures by mark.

Use the extras. In the appendices, you'll find a decision tree to help you determine whether you can proceed with a notarization, a pricing worksheet, and a glossary of medical and legal terms in plain English. These tools are designed to accompany you to every appointment.

Most of all, use this guide as a companion, not just a manual. You may be walking into a healthcare facility room alone, but this book will help make sure you're always prepared.

PART I:
THE PRACTICE

THE COMPASSIONATE NOTARY

UNDERSTANDING THE ENVIRONMENTS

Before you can serve effectively as a bedside notary, you need to understand the complex ecosystems you'll be entering. Each type of medical facility operates with distinct rhythms, regulations, and patient populations that directly impact your notarization process. This chapter introduces you to the four main facility types you'll encounter and explains why this knowledge is essential for successful appointments. Understanding these environments helps you schedule appropriately, communicate with staff effectively, and anticipate the challenges that could affect your signer's ability to complete their documents. Notarizing at a hospital or skilled nursing facility is unlike any other kind of appointment. It requires more than knowing how to fill out your certificate or verify a valid ID. It requires situational awareness, sensitivity, and a solid understanding of the facility type and its operations. It's essential that you understand how these factors affect your client and your work.

You are not always hired by the signer directly. Your customer might be a family member, a friend, or even a hospital staff member trying to assist a patient in completing urgent paperwork. That means from the moment you accept the call, you need to assess not just the legalities of notarization but also the human dynamics and environmental considerations that could impact whether the job gets done and the way it gets done.

Let's start by getting clear on the four main types of facilities you'll encounter: general hospitals (acute care facilities), long-term specialty care hospitals, skilled nursing facilities, and hospice facilities.

1. GENERAL HOSPITALS (ACUTE CARE FACILITIES)

These are large, licensed institutions staffed with physicians, nurses, and medical professionals offering 24-hour care. They handle a wide range of cases, including trauma, surgeries, and sudden medical conditions. Your signer may be in a private room or a shared space divided by curtains. Because hospital stays are often short-term, there's often a sense of urgency—documents may need to be signed before a procedure, a transfer, or discharge.

General hospitals typically include:
- Emergency departments
- Intensive care units
- Medical-surgical units
- Labor and delivery wards

Notaries working in these environments need to consider timing carefully. The signer/patient may be in and out of tests or heavily medicated, which can affect their ability to sign. Expect interruptions and allow extra time to navigate the hospital layout.

2. LONG-TERM SPECIALTY CARE HOSPITALS

Specialty care hospitals serve patients with complex, ongoing medical needs that can't be met in a traditional hospital or home setting. These facilities are equipped to care for patients on ventilators, receiving dialysis, IV medications, or other intensive therapies—even if the patient is no longer considered "acute."

You may find signers here who are medically stable but physically fragile, with limited communication abilities. These facilities are often quieter and more controlled than general hospitals, but appointments still require flexibility and compassion.

3. SKILLED NURSING FACILITIES (SNFS)

These inpatient centers provide short-term rehab or long-term daily care. Signers here may be recovering from surgeries, transfer from hospital stay, chronic illness, or other conditions that require occupational, physical, or speech therapy. Others may be permanent residents who need help with daily living due to chronic disease or cognitive decline.

Staff at SNFs are often more available and familiar with notary needs, but the following barriers may still be present:
- Medication schedules
- Language barriers
- Shared rooms with little privacy
- Staff are not allowed to witness documents

Understanding the roles of staff, such as certified nursing assistants (CNAs), therapists, and social workers, can help you coordinate more effectively upon arrival. Additionally, in many states, the Advance Health Care Directive requires that an ombudsman meet with the signer before notarization to ensure capacity and confirm the choice of their Agent.

Why This Knowledge Matters

Each facility type has its own unique rhythm and sets of rules. Knowing how each of these institutions operates will help you in these matters:
- Schedule your appointments with better timing
- Set realistic expectations for the signer
- Communicate more effectively with staff
- Respect the patient's medical and emotional state

Above all, possessing this knowledge will prepare you to serve with dignity and professionalism, even in the most challenging environments.

4. HOSPICE FACILITIES

You may be asked to come to a facility that specializes in the care of those diagnosed as terminal and have an estimated time of less than six months to live. Of course, some patients may have more time than that, depending on their condition. And unfortunately, many have much less, as some wait till the last days to seek out hospice care. In this case, it is usually too late for notarization due to medication; however, there is always an exception. Hospice care can also be a wing in a skilled nursing facility or hospital. What is different is their care plan, which is palliative or "comfort care."

SUMMARY: UNDERSTANDING THE ENVIRONMENTS

Hospitals and skilled care facilities are complex institutions with varying policies and protocols that affect your access, timing, and the notarial act itself. From general acute care hospitals to long-term specialty and skilled nursing facilities, knowing where you're going and what that means for your appointment is the first step to success.

KEY TAKEAWAYS

→ General hospitals treat a wide range of acute conditions with short-term stays.

→ Specialty hospitals provide specialized long-term care for specific conditions.

→ Skilled nursing facilities provide rehabilitative and long-term care without hospitalization.

→ Hospice takes care of patients who are terminal and typically at end of life.

→ Each setting poses similar challenges: unpredictable schedules, shared rooms, and procedural protocols.

→ Understanding facility flow, like parking, check-in, and navigating the halls, is crucial to managing time and expectations effectively.

CHAPTER 2

A DAY IN THE LIFE

Before diving into procedures and protocols, you need to see what bedside notarization looks like in practice. The following scenarios walk you through two real-world appointments from initial phone calls to completion—one in a skilled nursing facility and one in a hospital setting. These examples illustrate how the concepts from Chapter 1 play out in real time and preview the skills you'll develop throughout this book. Pay attention to how each scenario handles intake questions, facility navigation, signer assessment, and the unexpected challenges that arise. These aren't theoretical exercises—they represent the kinds of appointments you'll encounter regularly as a bedside notary.

It's just after 10 am when the adult son calls. His mother is in a skilled nursing facility recovering from a fall, and they need an advance health care directive signed so he can help make medical decisions should she not be able to do so herself in the future.

He sounds calm but unsure of what's required. I explain that in **many long-term care facilities**, an **ombudsman**—a state-certified patient advocate must be present to act as a **special witness** for this type of document. Their job is to ensure the resident is signing willingly, understands the document, and agrees with the choice of the individual being named as their agent.

He hadn't heard of that requirement, so I directed him to the SNF's social worker, who can usually coordinate the ombudsman's visit. I'm happy to coordinate if needed, but we've agreed that he'll follow up and then call me back to schedule once he confirms a time.

PREPARING FOR THE VISIT

Later that day, the son confirms the ombudsman will meet us at 3 pm

Before I leave, I verify:
- The **document is complete** and has the proper notarial wording
- The **signer has a valid ID**
- The **signer is alert, able to communicate, and can sign unaided**
- I note that a **special witness section** is included for the ombudsman's signature

In my notary bag, I double-check my essentials:
- Journal and ID form
- Multiple pens
- Clipboards
- PPE and sanitizer
- Extra acknowledgement and jurat certificates, just in case

AT THE FACILITY

I arrive early to navigate the parking and check-in procedures. Skilled nursing facilities often have multiple wings, so I leave extra time to find the right building and room.

The ombudsman arrives just before 3 pm. We meet at the nurse's station, confirm the resident is available, and walk back together.

The signer—an older woman in a shared room—is sitting up in bed and smiles when I introduce myself. I explain who I am, what I'm there to do, and the ombudsman introduces herself and explains her role as the patient's advocate.

The ombudsman begins with her own set of questions:
- Do you understand that you are naming someone to help make medical decisions for you?
- Is this what you want?
- Do you feel pressured by anyone to sign this?

Once the ombudsman is satisfied that the signer is **alert, aware, and willing**, she gives me the go-ahead.

I verify the signer's ID, check the notarial wording on the document, and ask my own orientation questions:
- Can you tell me your full name?
- Do you understand what this document is?
- Are you signing this because you want to?

She signs slowly but confidently. The ombudsman signs the special witness section, and I complete the notarization.

AFTER THE APPOINTMENT

I will make a **detailed journal entry** noting these details:
- That an ombudsman was present and signed as required
- The signer's responses and demeanor
- Time of appointment and name of the person who contacted me
- That the document was completed without issue

Before I leave, I thank the ombudsman and the son, who had joined via video call during the signing. I offer a business card for future referrals and head back to the car.

This wasn't just notarization; it was a legal and emotional moment in a family's care journey. Being calm, prepared, and respectful made all the difference.

A DAY IN THE LIFE FOR HOSPITAL

To help a notary who has not handled a hospital assignment here is what it could look like.

A DAY IN THE LIFE OF A BEDSIDE NOTARY - HOSPITAL

It's 9:15 am when the call comes in.

The woman on the line is calling from out of state, her father is in a rehab facility following surgery, and they need a power of attorney signed today. She sounds hopeful, nervous, and a little rushed.

I take a deep breath, smile (yes, they can hear it), and begin asking my intake questions. *Does the signer have an ID?* Yes. *Is he alert and aware?* Most of the time. *Does he speak English, and can he communicate independently?* Yes. I ask to see a copy of the document. She texts over the signature page, and I confirm it has a proper notarial certificate.

By the time we're off the phone, I've confirmed everything I need: valid ID, completed document, and a signer who appears to meet the requirements. I scheduled the appointment for 12:30 pm, allowing myself buffer time to handle any potential delays.

Preparing for the Visit

I check that my notary bag is loaded with the usual supplies:
- Clipboard
- Extra pens (regular and easy grip)
- Journal and ID check sheet
- Masks, sanitizer, gloves
- A small bottle of water—for me

I arrive at the facility and park across the street in a visitor garage. After walking through a metal detector, checking in with security, and navigating the elevator maze to the third floor, I stop at the nurse's station to announce my visit. The nurse nods and says, *He just finished lunch—should be a good time.*

At the Bedside

The patient's daughter is on speakerphone, and he's awake when I enter. I introduce myself, explain what I'm here to do, and sit beside him at eye level.

I begin with orientation questions: *I am Laura, your notary today.*

Please tell me your name.

Can you tell me where you are?

Can you tell me who is on the speakerphone with you?

Are you expecting to sign a document? Do you know what this document is about? If you have difficulty naming it, can you provide a brief description?

He answers all of them clearly and without hesitation. I note this in my journal.

He shows me his ID, which is still valid and matches the name on the document. I will review the certificate again. Everything checks out. I hand him a pen, and he signs it slowly.

It takes a little longer than usual, but I'm in no rush. I notarize the document, scan it with my mobile app for his daughter, and thank him warmly.

Wrapping Up

I make a detailed journal entry with the required elements while the event is still fresh in my mind. In addition, I note:
- Screening results
- Reason for the significant discrepancy in his signature
- Names of family members in attendance
- Name of the person who hired me

It's not always this smooth. Sometimes you walk away. Sometimes emotions run high. But today it worked. And that's why I do this work, to make a complicated moment a little easier for someone else.

These scenarios demonstrate what bedside notarization looks like in practice—but success in these environments requires more than just watching others navigate them. Before you accept your first medical facility appointment, you need to ensure you have the foundational notarial competence that makes everything else possible.

CHAPTER 3

WHAT EVERY NOTARY SHOULD KNOW

Competence before the call

Bedside notarizations carry higher stakes and greater risks than typical mobile appointments. The documents you'll notarize often involve life-altering decisions about property, healthcare, and legal authority, frequently executed by vulnerable individuals in emotionally charged situations. This chapter establishes the foundational knowledge you must have before accepting your first hospital assignment. Without this competency base, you risk legal liability, failed appointments, and potential harm to the very people you're trying to serve. You must be certain that you have the **foundational knowledge** to perform notarial acts confidently, legally, and professionally. This environment does not tolerate guesswork.

WHY FOUNDATIONAL TRAINING MATTERS

Medical facilities are not the place to "learn as you go." Mistakes in these settings carry greater risks—both to the signer and to you as a notary. If you're a new notary or haven't had formal training, it's **imperative** to complete your state's official notary education if available. If your state does not require training, consider taking a reliable foundational course, such as Notary Essentials by the National Notary Association, or an equivalent. These courses teach core duties and procedures that must become second nature before entering complex, emotionally charged environments, such as hospitals, skilled nursing facilities, or hospice facilities.

KNOW THE ACTS YOU'LL BE PERFORMING

These are the most common notarial acts for signatures you'll encounter in medical settings:

- **Acknowledgment** You verify the signer's identity and confirm they are willingly signing the document. The signer may sign before your arrival or in your presence, but they must acknowledge to you that they signed it.
- **Jurat (AKA oath upon verification)** This notarial act requires personal appearance, identity verification, and an **oath or affirmation** that the content of the document is true. The signer must sign in your presence.
- **Signature Witnessing** You verify the identity of the signer, and you must witness the signature of the principal.

All acts require focus, attention to detail, and a clear understanding of state-specific rules for certificates, identification, and procedures for handling exceptions to identification requirements:

- **Signature by mark:** a signature accommodation to use a mark instead of a signature. It may be anything the signer can produce and is allowed in most states.
- **Use of credible witnesses:** This is an alternative method of identification when the signer does not have a state-approved identification card.

The accommodation described here represents common practices, but requirements vary significantly by state. Before using signature by mark or credible witnesses, verify your state's specific requirements for witness qualifications, journal entries, and certificate wording.

WHY BEDSIDE NOTARIZATIONS CARRY MORE RISK

Documents signed in medical facilities are often **heavily contested** later. Common examples of these documents include the following.

- Power of Attorney
- Advance Health Care Directive or Living Will
- Last Will and Testament
- Deed transferring real estate

- Entire living trust package

These are powerful legal documents, some granting other people legal rights over money, property, or healthcare decisions. You must handle these documents with professional care and unimpeachable notarial execution.

OUR CORE MISSION AS NOTARIES

Always remember: our mission is **not** to approve or advise on the content of a document. Our role is to **verify identity** and ensure the signer is **signing willingly, not under duress, and that they're aware** of the contents of the document. The public depends on us to protect them in their most vulnerable moments.

That responsibility begins with competence. If you're not yet confident in your notarial knowledge, take the time to get trained with a reputable instructor before accepting your first bedside appointment. You and your clients deserve that.

CHAPTER 4

INTAKE AND PRESCREENING

Your first defense

Your success—or failure—as a bedside notary is largely determined before you ever leave your house. The intake call is your first line of defense against failed appointments, legal complications, and situations that put vulnerable signers at risk. This chapter teaches you how to conduct thorough prescreening that protects both you and your signer while setting clear expectations for everyone involved. Master these intake skills, and you'll dramatically reduce your no-go appointments while building trust with families during their most stressful moments.

The facility appointment often begins with a phone call, not from the signer, but from a family member, friend, hospital staff, or legal professional. That initial call sets the tone for everything that follows. Asking the right questions at the outset saves time, prevents frustration, and, most importantly, protects you and the signer from attempting a notarization that cannot proceed legally or ethically.

In this chapter, we'll walk through the way to confidently and compassionately manage that first call, essential questions to ask, and the way to document it. You need to arrive fully prepared, with a clear understanding of the situation.

YOU MAY BE TALKING TO ANYONE—BUT THE SIGNER IS THE FOCUS

The person calling you may be any one of these:

- A concerned adult child
- A hospital case manager
- A lawyer's assistant
- A friend is trying to help
- A spouse or caregiver

Your legal duty, though, is to the signer. That's why every intake call should focus on gathering the information needed to evaluate:
- Whether the signer can meet the legal requirements for notarization
- What type of document is to be signed
- What support or tools might be required
- Whether the job should be scheduled at all

USE AN INTAKE FORM

Having a structured intake form allows you to collect consistent and complete information, helping to ensure that you don't forget critical details in the moment. This form can be paper, digital, or even a checklist in your notes app. I have created a sample form at the back of this book to get you started.

Key sections should include:
- Name of caller and relationship to signer
- Facility name, address, and room number
- The best contact number for updates
- Type of document(s) to be signed
- Whether witnesses are required
- Whether the current identification is available for the signer
- Ability of the signer to communicate and sign
- Willingness to provide document preview
- Fee agreement and payment method

PRESCREENING QUESTIONS THAT MATTER

1. Is the signer alert and aware at this moment?

Ask the caller:

Is the signer awake, aware, and able to hold a conversation right now?

If the answer is *not sure*, suggest they check with the nursing staff. If the signer is not alert and oriented, notarization must wait.

2. Can the signer communicate directly with the notary without assistance?

This question is critical.

Ask the caller: *Can the signer speak or otherwise communicate directly with me without someone else helping them answer?*

Communication doesn't have to be verbal; it can include writing, head nods, or gestures, as long as it's direct and unassisted. If the caller says they usually have to *translate* the signer's responses or that the signer can't respond clearly, that's a red flag, and you should consider stopping the signing.

3. Does the signer speak and understand the language I use?

Notarization requires clear and direct communication between the notary and the signer; however, in most states, the document can be in a foreign language, as it is not the notary's responsibility to vet the document beyond its completion. (It is the notary's job to ensure that there are no blank spaces or missing pages.)

Ask: *Does the signer speak and understand English (or your language, if different)?*

If the answer is no, you must find a notary who speaks the signer's language. You can use Google Translator to inform them that they need another notary, or you must arrange an alternative legal solution. Using a family member or nurse as an interpreter is not acceptable.

4. Can the signer sign their name unassisted?

Some signers may have weaknesses, tremors, or limited mobility, but **they must still be able to sign voluntarily and independently**.

Ask: *Can the signer physically sign their name unassisted, with no one else guiding their hand?*

If they can't write their full signature but can make a mark, such as an "X," that may still be acceptable in many states, but you'll need to know your local law and whether additional witnesses are required.

5. What is the document?

Ask: *What type of document is it—power of attorney, advance health care directive, trust paperwork? Is the document filled out and ready for signature, or is it still being completed?*

Then ask: *If you are willing, would you email or text me a photo of the document—at least the signature page with the notary wording—so I can confirm it is something I can notarize?*

Reviewing the document ahead allows you to preview its completeness and notarial viability before accepting the job, saving everyone time and preventing frustration.

6. What form of ID does the signer have?

Ask for the **type and condition** of identification: *Does the signer have an original photo ID, such as a driver's license, state ID, or passport?*

If they don't have one that meets your state requirements, ask if **credible witnesses** are available and willing to appear and swear to the signer's identity. Explain to the caller what that entails.

7. Will witnesses be required?

Some documents, such as advance directives or estate planning documents, require witnesses in addition to or instead of a notary.

Ask: *Does the document require witnesses?*

If yes, explain clearly: *Most facilities do not allow their staff to act as witnesses. Prepare the signer or their family to provide **disinterested witnesses**; these are people not named in the document, nor will they benefit from it.*

*If the family cannot arrange witnesses, you can offer to provide them **as a separate, paid service.***

FEE STRUCTURE AND PAYMENT EXPECTATIONS

Be transparent about your fee structure. Include:
- Travel fee
- Wait time
- **Any additional fees** (e.g., for witnesses or late-night appointments)

Also, confirm: *I accept [cash, card, mobile payment apps.*

Then, set expectations: *Once I arrive at the facility, even if we cannot complete the notarization because the signer doesn't qualify or isn't able to sign, the **travel fee is still due.** I'll make every effort to verify in advance that I can complete the appointment, and I appreciate your understanding.*

It protects your time and professionalism while giving the caller a fair warning.

✦ **TIP:** Make it easy for your customer to pay you!

FINAL NOTE: SET EXPECTATIONS UPFRONT

Before ending the call, clearly summarize your conversation:
- What you'll need from them (ID, witnesses, completed docs)
- Whether they'll send over a photo of the document
- When and how their payment is collected
- You may cancel or reschedule on-site if legal requirements aren't met

SAMPLE SCRIPT FOR THE CALLER

Thank you for calling. Before I schedule, I would like to ask a few questions to ensure I understand the signer's awareness, ability to sign, and the type of document we're working with. If it's okay, I'd also like you to send me a photo of the signature page and notary certificate. These questions help me prepare and make sure we don't schedule a notarization appointment that can't be completed.

SAMPLE to summarize once you know the details of the job and what you and your customer have agreed to:

Mr. Customer, let me make sure I have this right. I'll meet you at Memorial Hospital, Room #611, at 3 pm tomorrow, the 12th. We'll be finalizing the power of attorney and an advance healthcare directive, and we've agreed on the price—my quote of $105 based on what you described. The payment will be with Zelle, and you've confirmed that she is alert and aware. I will be asking her several questions directly to confirm when I am there. She will have her current government-issued identification for the appointment, and she can sign unassisted. You have the documents, and they will be complete, so we just need to sign. Is all that correct? I want to remind you that if I am unable to complete notarization due to one of the requirements we discussed not being met, the travel fee will still apply. Then I look forward to meeting her and all of you. I will see you tomorrow.

IN SUMMARY

Doing prescreening is not just a time-saver; it's a professional safeguard. When you know what to ask and how to listen, you reduce your no-go appointments, protect the signer's rights, and build trust with those seeking your service. You may not meet your signer until you walk into that hospital room, but your first impression starts **with the phone call**.

INTAKE AND PRESCREENING – GETTING THE PHONE CALL

Effective screening begins the moment the phone rings. Whether the caller is the signer, a family member, or staff, your questions determine whether the job is doable, legal, and compensated. Asking the right questions up-front protects your time and ensures a smoother appointment.

KEY TAKEAWAYS

→ Confirm that the signer can communicate directly, speak your language, and sign unassisted.

→ Ask what document needs to be notarized and request a photo or scan of the signature page.

→ Confirm whether the document includes notarial wording; if not, the signer must direct which certificate to use.

→ Ask if an acceptable ID is available or if they will need credible witnesses.

→ Inquire about witness requirements; most facilities do not pro-vide them.

→ Set clear expectations for travel and notarization fees, including any additional costs that may apply if travel is required but the appointment does not result in a notarized document.

→ Use an intake form to ensure you cover all necessary questions and document responses.

CHAPTER 5

PROTECTING YOURSELF

Your safety net

Bedside notarizations carry higher liability risks than typical mobile work due to vulnerable signers, contested documents, and emotionally charged family dynamics. Your professional protection depends on consistent procedures, thorough documentation, and knowing your legal limits. This chapter outlines essential strategies for safeguarding your notarial practice, from maintaining detailed journals to carrying appropriate insurance to building a support network of experienced mentors. These protective measures allow you to serve confidently in high-stakes environments without compromising your livelihood or commission.

Notarizing in medical settings is deeply rewarding but also carries a higher level of risk than many other assignments. You're dealing with vulnerable signers, emotionally charged families, and high-stakes documents. While your mission is to serve, your **responsibility is to protect** both the signer and you.

This chapter outlines the key ways to safeguard your notarial practice—legally, professionally, and ethically.

USE OF REASONABLE CARE

Your strongest shield is **consistency**. Create a process that helps you assess, document, and walk away when things don't meet legal standards.
- Follow your intake script every time; screen for ID, willingness, comprehension, and ability to sign.

- Document **everything**, especially if you refuse or discontinue the appointment. Include the name of the person who called, what was observed, and why you made the decision.
- If you suspect coercion, confusion, or undue influence, **trust your instincts** and stop the signing.

✦ Tip: Your journal is your memory and legal backup. Think of it as your insurance on paper.

KNOW YOUR LEGAL LIMITS

Not all accommodation is legal in every state. Know what's allowed—and what's not—**before** you're asked to improvise bedside.

Check your state's laws regarding:
- Signature by Mark
- Signature by proxy
- Use of interpreters for deaf and hard-of-hearing signers
- Blind Signers
- Alternative forms of identification
- Remote online notarization, which may have document limitations, such as Last Wills

As a notary, you have state laws to follow. If your state doesn't allow a requested method, politely decline and explain that you're required to follow state law. Be prepared to consult an attorney, Legal Shield (if you have membership), or a Legal Document Assistant (LDA) if a more suitable solution is available. Remember that for physical disabilities such as blindness, inability to sign their name, and others, there are Federal ADA laws that require reasonable accommodation for those with disabilities.

RELIABLE RESOURCES TO STAY CURRENT

The resources I list are based on my direct experience. None has sponsored my endorsement.

Laws and procedures can change. Subscribe, follow, or bookmark these reliable sources to stay up to date:
- Your state's notary handbook is essential reading for all notaries.
- Secretary of State website for email alerts, updates, or new legislation.
- National Notary Association (NNA) website page; Knowledge Center
- **NNA Hotline:** available to NNA members for notary guidance.
- California League of Independent Notaries (CLIN): offers nationwide updates and advocacy.

ERRORS & OMISSIONS INSURANCE (E&O)

Mistakes happen. And even if they don't, you can still be sued.

E&O insurance covers unintentional errors and legal defense costs. It does not cover:
- Fines or penalties from your Secretary of State
- Willful misconduct
- Unauthorized legal advice

Not all polices are the same. The National Notary Association recommends getting a **$25,000** policy (outside the loan signing specialty), based on historical averages for notary-related claims.

Look for a policy that includes **"tail coverage,"** which protects you even after your commission expires, **if the policy was active at the time of the notarization** in question.

> ✦ **TIP:** Even if your state does not require E&O insurance, it's one of the most affordable forms of professional protection you can carry.

MENTORSHIP MATTERS

Don't go alone. A trusted mentor or experienced colleague can help you make the right call-in uncertain situations.

Ways to build your support network:

- Ask a seasoned notary you respect to be a resource.
- Consider working with an NNA Ambassador who has experience in your specialty.
- Online Notary Skill Training Courses
- **www.CoachMeLaura.com**
  - » **Advanced notary training videos**
  - » Laura's Inner Circle, hosted by Coach me Laura
  - » Free consult **www.calendly.com/biewer**
  - » California Advanced Notary Training
  - » LBP Video Replay Library: includes POA, Advanced health care directive, and Last Will document review
- **National Notary Association**
  - » Essentials online tutorial
- Join professional organizations like the
  - » National Notary Association
  - » American Society of Notaries
  - » California League of Independent Notaries
- **Join a trusted community.**
  - » TNT (Tuesday Notary Titans), sponsored by Marketing4notaries/ CoachMeLaura
  - » NotaryCoach.com
  - » Vetted Facebook Groups - State-specific are best, and upon recommendation by trusted source
  - » Monday General Mentorship, hosted by Notary Stars
  - » Attend an in-person or online notary seminar for advanced training
  - » NotaryFamily.com
- Local in-person or online notary events
  - » NNA Annual Conference
- Read books on notary-related topics of interest:
  - » Beyond Loan Signings – Bill Soroka, Laura Biewer
  - » On the Move, 5 Step Relationship Driven Marketing Plan- Jen Neitzel

SUMMARY

Notaries can protect themselves legally, professionally, and ethically when working in high-risk, emotionally sensitive environments. Key strategies include following consistent intake and documentation procedures, knowing state laws and limits, staying informed through reliable resources, carrying E&O insurance, and building a trusted mentorship and professional support network. These safeguards help notaries serve confidently while minimizing risk.

You'll gain confidence, avoid costly mistakes, and be able to serve with clarity—even in the most complex bedside situations.

Providing notary services in hospitals and skilled nursing facilities requires more than just knowing where to park or how to verify identification. It's an act of professionalism, empathy, and trustworthiness. Your reputation will not only get you hired, but it will also get you **invited back** and **recommended to others**.

KEY TAKEAWAYS

→ Protect yourself by developing and following a clear, consistent process for all bedside notarizations.

→ Know what your state allows and where to draw the line on accommodations.

→ Document thoroughly, especially when walking away from notarization.

→ Invest in E&O insurance that includes tail coverage and be clear about what it does (and doesn't) protect.

→ Utilize official resources and establish a trusted mentor network to stay informed and supported.

CHAPTER 6

WHEN TO WALK AWAY

Discontinuing a signing

In Chapter 5, you learned how to protect yourself through documentation, insurance, and professional practices. But sometimes protection means declining or stopping notarization altogether..."Knowing when to refuse or discontinue a notarization is as important as knowing how to complete one. Medical facility environments present numerous scenarios where proceeding would be legally inappropriate or ethically wrong, despite family pressure or urgent circumstances. This chapter teaches you to recognize red flags, make difficult decisions with confidence, and communicate refusals professionally. Your willingness to walk away when necessary, protects vulnerable signers and demonstrates the integrity that builds long-term professional success.

Discontinuing a signing isn't failure; it's a mark of your integrity and your understanding of the law and ethics involved. This chapter guides us when and how to professionally walk away from a signing that cannot proceed.

1. THE SIGNER FAILS AWARENESS OR WILLINGNESS TEST

It's time to stop the process if the signer shows any of these types of behaviors:

- Cannot answer basic orientation questions, such as, What is your name? Where are you? What are you signing?
- Is heavily medicated, incoherent, unresponsive, unconscious, and yes, in a coma
- Appears pressured or confused

- Does not seem to understand the document or their actions

Even if family members insist that the signer is "fine," **you must observe this yourself**. Your duty is to the **signer's clarity and autonomy**, not the convenience of others.

> ✦ Tip: It helps to say, as a notary, *I am required to ensure the signer understands and is signing willingly. I'm not comfortable moving forward today.*

2. IDENTIFICATION DOESN'T MEET LEGAL STANDARDS

You cannot proceed with the notarization in these cases:
- The ID has expired beyond your state's acceptable timeframe.
- The name on the ID does not match the name on the document, and they do not have an alternative method to verify it.
- The ID is missing altogether, and no credible witnesses are present or available.
- The ID is a form that your state does not permit. (picture on phone, photocopy. extension)
- **Best Practice:** Verify their ID status during the intake call to avoid unnecessary travel or misunderstandings, including the type and name on the ID vs the document.

A good guideline from the NNA and the most conservative approach is this: if the name on the document is "equal to or less than" the name on the ID, it is acceptable as long as the other elements appear to match the signer. However, be aware that there can be name variations, such as nicknames, use or lack of middle names, and you may decide to allow it. Here is my recommendation: **You are the notary in the chair**.
- Are there other details on the ID that can help you confirm their identity, such as eye color, height, date of birth, or address details?
- Does the signer have additional forms of ID in their wallet that support the name? You will need to make that decision based on several factors:
- Location: Are you in their home or meeting at a public place?
- Type of document: Is it transferring ownership of property or giving rights to another, or is it extending their benefits?

- The amount of variation between the ID and the person you are meeting.

3. THE DOCUMENT CANNOT BE NOTARIZED

Sometimes, the signer or family presents a document that is not valid as is:
- It's incomplete
- It lacks notarial wording
- It contains a notarial act that is not permitted in your state
- You cannot determine the type of certificate from the wording provided

If the signer cannot clarify the appropriate certificate (e.g., jurat vs. acknowledgment) and there is **no direction from the client**, you must **not choose it for them**.

You may offer to do this:
- Explain the types of **notarial certificates** in plain language, and ask the signer to choose one
- Contact the document's issuing party, preparer, or receiving agency
- **Reschedule** the signing

4. REQUIRED WITNESSES ARE NOT AVAILABLE

If the document requires one or more **disinterested witnesses**, and:
- None are present
- The ones available are family members or beneficiaries
- The facility prohibits staff from serving as witnesses
- And the caller is unprepared; **you must not proceed**.

You can offer to:
- Reschedule
- Bring paid witnesses
- **Provide a resource list** for locating witnesses
- Seek out other patients' visitors who might be willing to witness

But do not proceed with a partial or invalid signing.

5. INTERFERENCE OR HOSTILE ENVIRONMENT

You suspect the signer is being coerced. Even if a signer appears alert and aware, they may still be under pressure from others. It is your duty to ensure their willingness is authentic and unpressured. These situations have red flags:

- Someone else answers on behalf of the signer, people talk over the signer, and the signer looks for approval before signing
- You're **unable** to speak with the signer privately. Always ask to talk with the signer alone and use open-ended questions, such as: Are you signing this because you want to? Do you understand what this document is for?
- The atmosphere feels tense, and family members seem rushed or emotionally charged.
- Someone becomes **angry** or **pressures** you to move forward

If you suspect the signer is not acting voluntarily, **stop the notarization immediately**. Document your observations in your journal and leave professionally.

You can say:

I'm going to stop this signing for now. I'm happy to reschedule when the environment is more appropriate for proper notarization.

6. HOW TO LOG A DISCONTINUED SIGNING

Whether your state requires a notary journal or not, you should document these facts:

- The date and time, the name of the signer
- The **reason for discontinuation** (e.g., signer unaware, lack of ID, incomplete doc)
- Name of the person who called for the appointment
- Any notable conversations or behaviors

This documentation protects you in the event of a complaint or legal inquiry.

7. TRAVEL FEE AND COMMUNICATION

If your intake process is clear and professional, you should already have stated:
- **When** a travel fee is owed (e.g., upon arrival, regardless of completion)
- **How** can it be paid (e.g., credit card, Venmo, Zelle, check, cash)
- Some or all of the travel fee is **nonrefundable** if the notarization cannot proceed due to signer or document issues.

It is perfectly professional to say:

Although we couldn't complete the notarization today, I will charge a travel fee for the visit, as previously discussed. I can provide a receipt for your records.

> ✦ **TIP:** Know before you go! Text or email the requirements for the assignment and qualifications for the signer.

8. WALKING AWAY IS SOMETIMES THE MOST PROFESSIONAL ACT

This chapter isn't about how to **avoid** jobs; it's about protecting yourself, your commission, and, most importantly, the signer's rights and dignity.

Having strong prescreening practices and using your best judgment on-site will help you in these ways:
- Reduce failed appointments
- Protect vulnerable signers
- Build a strong reputation for professionalism.

9. WHEN NOT TO PROCEED

Even when the appointment is scheduled, documents are in hand, and everyone is eager to proceed, sometimes the answer still must be no. Recognizing when to pause or walk away is a hallmark of notarial integrity.

KEY TAKEAWAYS

→ Arrive with compassion but lead with clarity.

→ Clearly explain your role as a neutral witness, not an advocate or advisor.

→ Build in extra time and prepare emotionally.

→ Be willing to walk away if the signer does not meet capacity standards—even if the family disagrees.

CHAPTER 7

SCHEDULING WITH SENSITIVITY

The medical facility eco system

Medical facilities don't operate on business hours, they run on medication schedules, shift changes, and the unpredictable rhythms of patient care. Scheduling bedside notarization requires understanding this complex ecosystem and timing your arrival for maximum success. This chapter shows you how to work within medical facility operations, avoid common scheduling pitfalls, and build buffer time for the unexpected delays that are inevitable in healthcare settings. Proper scheduling demonstrates respect for the care environment and significantly improves your completion rate.

Once you've completed a successful intake call and confirmed that a notarization may proceed, your next challenge is scheduling. At first glance, this might seem simple—pick a time and write it down; however, in bedside notarizations, scheduling is a dynamic skill. You're navigating shifting medical routines, emotional family dynamics, and logistical realities.

This chapter will help you choose the **right time**, manage expectations, and avoid common scheduling pitfalls, so you arrive at the facility as a welcomed professional, not an added stressor.

UNDERSTAND THE ENVIRONMENT YOU'RE ENTERING

Hospitals and skilled nursing facilities are not 9-to-5 offices. They are 24/7 ecosystems with these operations:
- Nurses change shifts (often around 7 am and 7 pm)
- Medications are dispensed on schedules that may affect awareness

- Procedures (e.g., x-rays, therapy, lab draws) can delay or interrupt appointments
- Meals are delivered at fixed times, and rooms can become busy

Best Times to Schedule

- **Mid-morning (9:30 am–11:30 am)** is often ideal. Patients are awake, have had breakfast, and morning medications have been administered.
- **Early afternoon (1:00–3:00 pm)** can also work, as it's typically after lunch and before fatigue or afternoon treatments set in. Of course, if the family cannot be there until after their work schedule, you will need to adjust your schedule accordingly.
- **Avoid** early mornings, mealtimes, and medication windows (ask when medications that impact their cognitive ability are dispensed).

Ask the caller: *Do you know when the patient is most alert and not scheduled for therapy, medication, or meals?*

Build in Extra Time

Unlike a straightforward signing in an office or café, bedside notarizations come with delays:
- It may take time to navigate the facility
- The signer may need time to sit up or get situated
- Interruptions from staff or family are common
- Orientation screening takes time and should never be rushed

Allow 30-45 minutes per hospital or SNF appointment, from arrival to departure from the parking lot, when one or a few documents are involved. For trust appointments, allow at least one hour.

You may only be notarizing one document, but the process and setting often require more flexibility. Living trust appointments typically have six to eight documents at most, and for one signer, my recommendation is sufficient; however, if there are two signers, add an additional 15 minutes.

LET THE CALLER KNOW: YOU'RE A GUEST IN THE CARE PLAN

Set expectations gently but clearly:

Even with an appointment, I may need to wait for medical staff to finish with the patient or pause if treatments are underway. I'll do my best to work efficiently, but I want to ensure it's safe and appropriate to proceed.

This builds trust and demonstrates that you respect the medical team's priorities and the signer's well-being.

HAVE A BACKUP PLAN

In some cases, a signer may unexpectedly:
- Become too drowsy or agitated to proceed
- Be moved to a different unit
- Refuse to sign

Prepare callers in advance: *If I arrive and the signer cannot proceed, I will document that, and we can reschedule. There will still be a travel fee since I reserved the time and made the visit.*

This clarity prevents discomfort or disputes later.

SAME-DAY APPOINTMENTS: TRIAGE WISELY

Sometimes, callers will say, *we need someone now.*

Suppose you're available, excellent! But never feel pressured to rush without conducting a proper intake.

Ask:
- Can you send a picture of the document first?
- Is the signer alert and aware?
- Can the facility accommodate me today?

Even urgent calls should meet the same standards for prescreening, readiness, and communication.

SAFETY FIRST FOR YOU AND THE SIGNER

Your safety matters, too. Consider this:
- Will it be dark by the time you leave?
- Is parking secure?
- Are there different entrance requirements during evening or late-night hours? Some hospitals limit access to certain doors or floors after hours and may require security escorts.

CONFIRM BEFORE YOU GO

Before heading out, do a final confirmation with the caller, as things can change. This confirmation doesn't have to be a live call; it could also be a text. You could prepare a text template on your cell phone to make it easy.
- Confirm time, patient's name, location, and **room number**
- Confirm availability of ID and witnesses, if needed
- Verify that documents are prepared and completed
- Confirm payment method

Create a simple confirmation text message:

Just confirming our 2 pm appointment at St. Mary's, room 614. The signer is John Smith, and the document is a POA. Two document witnesses are needed for this signing. Please ensure the document is completed, the signer's ID is available, and the required witnesses are in attendance. Thank you! Payment for the service will be made by credit card.

This communication serves as a final checkpoint for both parties, ensuring that time is not wasted.

> ✦ **TIP:** If they do not have the document they need, be prepared to suggest where they might find it, such as hospital social services or case management, which typically have health care directives or living wills. They can have a POA prepared by a paralegal/legal

document assistant (LDA), or they can download one from companies like these:

- Trust and Will for POAs, trusts, and last wills,
- Rocket Lawyer, LegalZoom, or
- Find a free PDF past the ads in the organic section (Typically Statutory wording)
- Office Max or other retail office supply stores

I have made friends with attorneys, LDAs, and shipping store staff, who have served as great resources in times like this.

SUMMARY: SCHEDULING WITH SENSITIVITY

Scheduling bedside notarization at a medical facility is more than plugging a time into your calendar. It's about thinking ahead, coordinating with the rhythm of medical care, and allowing space for the human elements that surround a difficult or emotional time. Being flexible yet assertive about your availability will help you serve your clients well without burning out.

When you approach scheduling with sensitivity, you become more than a notary; you become a trusted professional who is calm, prepared, and respected in the field.

When you're called to a medical facility, timing isn't just about your calendar—it's about honoring the rhythms of care.

KEY TAKEAWAYS

- → Ask about mealtimes, medication schedules, and nursing shift changes to choose the best visit window.
- → Avoid early mornings and late evenings unless it's urgent.
- → Be aware of the impact of medications that might impair alertness.
- → Allow generous time slots for bedside appointments, as these typically take longer than standard mobile assignments.
- → Clearly communicate the notary's limited role and authority to manage expectations.

CHAPTER 8

ENTERING THE FACILITY

From parking to the patient's room

Walking into a hospital or skilled nursing facility may seem straightforward—until you're the notary, navigating it solo with your bag, your tools, and the responsibility to complete a critical legal service. The path from parking lot to patient room can determine whether your appointment succeeds or fails before you even meet the signer. Navigation challenges, security protocols, and facility policies can derail even well-planned appointments if you're unprepared.

This chapter guides you through the practical logistics of facility entry, from parking strategies to security check-ins to finding the right room. Professional navigation skills not only save time, but they also establish credibility with staff who could become valuable referral sources.

STEP 1: PLAN FOR PARKING

Parking can be a time-consuming wildcard. Hospitals may have:
- Parking garages across the street or behind the building
- Designated visitor spaces may be several blocks away
- Limited or timed spaces
- Pay stations or validation kiosks

> ✦ **TIPS:**
> - **Arrive early**: Allow at least 15–20 extra minutes just for parking and check-in for first time at that facility.
> - **Note landmarks**: Some garages have color-coded or lettered levels. Take a photo so you can find your car again.

- Bring small bills or a credit card if parking isn't free.
- **Avoid loading zones** or ambulance lanes, even if it's just for a few minutes.

STEP 2: ENTRY PROCEDURES

After parking, you'll likely enter through a central lobby—but what happens next depends on the facility.

You may encounter:
- **Security check-ins**: ID required, name badge issued, visitor pass time-stamped
- **Metal detectors or bag searches**, especially in larger hospitals
- **Health Screenings:** This is still common in some SNFs
- **Electronic check-in kiosks:** require that you know the patient's name or room number

Be patient and courteous. These are protocols to protect vulnerable patients and the staff serving them.

STEP 3: GET THE RIGHT DIRECTIONS

Hospitals can feel like mazes. Wings labeled North, South, Tower A, or Pavilion 2 can be confusing without a guide.

How to navigate like a pro:
- Ask staff or security: Can you point me to [Unit or Room Number]?
- **There may be multiple buildings:** you might need to cross bridges or underground tunnels to get to the correct wing.
- Use the **correct elevator bank**. Some elevators only serve designated floors or departments.
- Watch for signs like "Staff Only" or "Authorized Personnel." Avoid entering these areas unless you are authorized personnel.

  ✦ **TIP:** Consider stopping at the nurse's desk to let them know you are there, why you are there, and whom you are seeing. Also, you might offer them a "leave behind" like a pen, biz cards, or other branded piece. And you might consider wearing a badge, which could be made from your own business card, making you look official and making check-in and navigation easier.

STEP 4: KNOW THE ROOM CONDITIONS

Once you find the right room, assess before you proceed:
- **Is protective gear required?** Look for signage indicating the required Personal Protective Equipment (PPE), such as masks, gloves, or full gowns.
- **Is it a shared room?** If so, the signer may have only partial privacy (just a curtain separating patients).
- **Is the medical staff present?** Wait respectfully for them to finish care tasks before beginning.

Keep this in mind: just because you've arrived, it doesn't mean you can start right away. This environment is centered on the patient's needs first, so be flexible.

STEP 5: ENTER WITH A PROFESSIONAL PRESENCE

Introduce yourself to the signer and to any family or caregivers who are present. A good opening line might be:

Hi, I'm Laura, the notary you scheduled for today. I'll need to ask for a few minutes with [signer's name] to confirm their willingness and awareness before we begin.

You are not a hospital staff member, but your demeanor and communication should be just as calm, clear, and respectful.

What to Bring Inside:
- Your notary **bag or organized tote** with notary tools
- **Clipboard:** don't rely on bedside tables, they may be cluttered or unusable
- Multiple working pens in black or blue ink, plus extras for gloved conditions

- Your photo ID card to get in
- Hand sanitizer or disinfecting wipes
- **Optional**: light snack or water in your car for afterward, especially if it's a long wait

> ✦ **TIP:** Have a weighted pen with a large barrel grip for those who have difficulty keeping the pen on paper or have gripping concerns due to arthritis or stroke.

> ✦ **TIP for document witnesses:** If they are not present, check for visitors, as that has been a successful way for me to get them. I usually ask family members to seek them out while I work with the signer.

EXIT CONSIDERATIONS

After your appointment:
- Record notes about the assignment in your journal before you leave, while fresh in your mind.
- Sign out at the visitor's desk or kiosk if required.
- Pay for or validate your parking. Keep the receipt for your records.
- Follow up with the signer (or contact person) via text or email to confirm completion. This could be a good time to ask for a review.
- If you have additional required tasks, such as dropping off at a courier or scanning back, handle those as soon as you have time. Remember that the job is not completed until you have finished all the requirements.

IN SUMMARY

The level of your professionalism is evident from the moment you arrive, as you perform your notarial duties, and in the way you navigate your environment. From parking lots to patient wings, your patience, preparedness, and presence make a difference. Clients (and facilities) will remember the notary who arrived on time, handled logistics with ease, and respected the setting they entered.

KEY TAKEAWAYS

→ Parking may be blocks away; build in walking time.

→ Evening visits? Ask about changes to entrance access and security.

→ Expect security check-ins and delays during busy visiting hours.

→ Request specific directions if you are unfamiliar with the facility.

→ Follow signage carefully; hospitals may have multiple towers or wings.

→ It's wise to announce your arrival at the nurse's station before entering the patient's room.

CHAPTER 9

SAFETY AND HYGIENE PROTOCOLS

Medical facilities house vulnerable populations with compromised immune systems, infectious diseases, and complex medical needs. As a visiting professional, you carry responsibility for both your safety and that of patients, families, and staff. This chapter outlines essential hygiene and safety protocols that protect everyone while maintaining your professional standards. Following these practices isn't just about health, it's about demonstrating the competence and care that will make you a trusted presence in medical settings.

Whether you're entering a general hospital, a long-term care facility, or a skilled nursing environment, your physical presence comes with responsibility—not just legal, but also hygienic. You are entering a space where patients are often vulnerable, immuno-compromised, or recovering from surgery or illness. Additionally, you'll be working closely with staff and family members, many of whom are navigating high-stress situations.

This chapter outlines how to protect **yourself**, **your signer**, and **your tools** while projecting professionalism and care that will make you a trusted presence in medical settings.

WHY HYGIENE MATTERS

A notary's first impression includes more than a polished appearance and confident voice. When entering a healthcare setting, it is also essential to be aware of infection control. Medical facilities have high standards for hygiene, and you should too, both for health reasons and to support your long-term reputation as a bedside notary.

NOTARY PERSONAL HYGIENE

Wash and sanitize your hands before and after every appointment. Carry hand sanitizer with at least 70% alcohol content and use it frequently if soap and water aren't available.

Avoid strong fragrances. Perfumes, colognes, or scented lotions can be overwhelming or even trigger allergic reactions in patients.

Dress appropriately. Comfortable, professional clothing that allows ease of movement is best. Always bring layers, a lightweight sweater or jacket you can remove if you need to put on protective gear. **Protective Equipment (PPE)**

Sometimes, bedside notarizations require **personal protective equipment**—even for brief visits. A clue is signage on the wall next to room entry and a cart with PPE.

A basic PPE kit includes:
- Disposable gloves
- A medical mask (N95 or surgical)
- Disposable gown

You may be asked to "garb up" if the patient is in isolation or under special precautions. If hospital staff provide you with PPE, follow their guidance. Remember, once you are garbed up and, in the room, do not go back outside with it on.

> ✦ **TIP:** Once you've used a pen or touched your journal while wearing gloves, **do not return those items to your bag** unless they've been sanitized. This is a good use for a **"leave-behind" pen.**

TOOL HYGIENE

Sanitize any tools you are using before and after your appointments in healthcare facilities.

Clipboard

Use a hard-surface clipboard that can be easily sanitized. Avoid leather-bound folders or porous materials. Wipe your clipboard with sanitizer before and after each use, especially if it comes in contact with the patient's bedding or tray.

Stamp

Wipe your notary stamp before and after every use. Avoid setting it on patient trays or bedside tables.

Journal (or e-Journal Device)

If using a tangible (**paper**) **journal**, either wrap the outside with plastic wrap like a book cover, which can be removed and discarded before leaving the room, or sanitize the cover and edges after each visit. Try to minimize the number of people who handle it.

Page protocol: If a signer touches the journal page, do not reuse it for your next appointment. Skip to a clean page to prevent the spread of germs between signers.

If using a **mobile device or tablet** for an e-journal, clean the screen with an alcohol-based wipe and remember the **electronic thumbprint glass on the device, too.**

Writing Supplies
- Always bring **several sanitized pens**, including one you're prepared to leave behind.
- Keep a few **special-grip pens** for signers who struggle with fine motor control or arthritis.
- Never assume the hospital or family will provide writing instruments, this is your responsibility as a professional.

SIGNING SPACE SANITATION

If the patient's environment is visibly unclean or cluttered, gently offer your clipboard or lapboard to maintain hygiene. Don't rely on the over-bed tray. It may be dirty, cluttered, or inaccessible; use your sanitized clipboard instead.

RESPECT FOR THE MEDICAL SETTING

Don't touch medical equipment—ever, even if it seems minor. Ask the nurse or staff for the patient currently receiving care before entering the room. I can look at the orientation sign on the wall in the room for name of nurse.

Be mindful that **shared rooms** mean limited privacy. Speak quietly and keep focus on your signer.

Please refrain from bringing food or drinks into patient areas.

If you feel unwell, **reschedule your appointment.** Your professional integrity includes not exposing vulnerable individuals to illness.

- If using a tangible (**paper) journal**, either wrap the outside with plastic wrap like a book cover, which can be removed and discarded before leaving the room, or sanitize the cover and edges after each visit. Try to minimize the number of people who handle it.
- **Page protocol:** If a signer touches the journal page, do not reuse it for your next appointment. Skip to a clean page to prevent the spread of germs between signers.
- If using a **mobile device or tablet** for an e-journal, clean the screen with an alcohol-based wipe and remember the **electronic thumbprint device, too.**

Signing Space Sanitation
- If the patient's environment is visibly unclean or cluttered, gently offer your clipboard or lapboard to maintain hygiene.
- Don't rely on the over-bed tray. It may be dirty, cluttered, or inaccessible; use your sanitized clipboard instead.

CLOSING THOUGHTS

Hygiene and infection awareness don't just protect health—they protect **your brand**. Being the notary who shows up prepared, who doesn't flinch at a gown-up requirement, and who handles their tools with care will earn you an invitation back. Hospitals, families, and even legal professionals will remember how you made a stressful situation easier and safer.

You are a guest in someone's healing space. Bring your skill, your compassion, and your sanitation wipes.

KEY TAKEAWAYS

→ Carry hand sanitizer, masks, and gloves.

→ Use sanitizing wipes on tools, such as the clipboard, stamp, pens, and the outside of your journal or device.

→ Avoid reusing touched journal pages—start fresh for each appointment.

→ Leave behind any pens used or be prepared to sanitize each one after signing.

→ Ask staff if any precautions, such as gowns and masks, are required.

Before putting pen to paper, ensure the signer is alert, aware, and willing to sign. Orientation is more than small talk—it's your professional assessment of the signer's capacity and consent. In healthcare settings, clarity around identity, intent, and understanding is crucial.

CHAPTER 10

ORIENTING THE SIGNER

Assessment is key to a willing and alert signer

The moment you begin interacting with your signer is when your legal responsibility truly begins. Unlike standard mobile appointments, bedside notarizations require careful assessment of signers who may be affected by medication, illness, or emotional distress. This chapter teaches you how to evaluate awareness, willingness, and capacity while maintaining the compassionate presence that vulnerable signers need. These orientation skills are your primary tool for ensuring legally valid notarizations while protecting signers from potential exploitation.

STEP-BY-STEP GUIDANCE:

1. **Introduce Yourself Clearly** and Greet the signer respectfully and state your role: Hi, my name is Laura, and I'm a notary public. I'm here to witness your signature on a legal document today.

    Ask Orientation Questions. These are not legal tests but indicators of alertness and awareness.

    Observe eye contact, but don't overinterpret. A signer's ability or willingness to make eye contact can offer insight into their comfort level, but it should not be used in isolation to assess willingness. Some individuals, especially those who are ill, elderly, or overwhelmed— may naturally avoid eye contact.

2. You might ask:
   » *Tell me your name?*
   » *Can you tell me where you are right now?*
   » *What document are we signing today?* If the signer struggles or is giving inconsistent answers, consider pausing to consult with nursing staff to determine if any medical condition, treatment, or medication may impair their ability to execute legal documents, especially those related to powers of attorney, healthcare directives, or deeds.

3. Check for willingness. **If you have concerns**:

   Ask for privacy (if others are present). *Before we proceed, I need just a few minutes alone with [signer's name] to speak privately. It's a standard part of my process to make sure I'm meeting legal requirements.*

   If there's resistance, **calmly reinforce the importance.** *I'm not permitted to continue unless I can speak directly and privately with the signer. Thank you for understanding.*

   Gently Assess for Coercion. Once alone with the signer, ask open-ended and non-leading questions in a warm, calm tone:
   » *Are you signing this of your own free will? Has anyone pressured you or told you that you must sign this? Do you feel comfortable proceeding with this notarization today?*
   » *Do you understand what this document will do after you sign it?*

4. **If you suspect coercion:**

   If the signer appears unsure, distressed, or hesitant, you should be aware of this: **Context matters more than first impressions.** Worry, hesitation, or nervousness may reflect the seriousness of the document or the weight of the decision, not necessarily coercion. Take time to observe the whole situation and ask thoughtful, open-ended questions before forming a conclusion. If you do believe the signer is being coerced, here is a script you can use to stop and exit.
   » *I appreciate your honesty. Based on what I'm seeing, I'm not comfortable proceeding with the notarization at this time. You must sign*

> *only when you feel completely ready and free to do so. If you would like to sign later, I can return.*
>
> » Explain to family members or others who are waiting: *The signer and I spoke, and at this time, I will not be completing the notarization. Should circumstances change, I can return. I appreciate your understanding.*

Although in most states, we notaries are not mandated reporters, it is our responsibility to safeguard vulnerable signers and uphold the trust placed in our profession. You may want to stop by the nurses' station or ask to speak to social services to inform them of what happened. They should be notified in case the family were to bring in another notary.

- **Verify ID or Witness Plan** Ask for the identification that the caller confirmed during intake. Ensure it meets your state's requirements; most states require government-issued photo identification. If their ID isn't available, implement your credible witness process as allowed by law.

  + **PRO TIP:** Keep a list of acceptable IDs and any specific requirements, such as a valid expiration date, photograph, and signature. You should also know whether a digital form of an ID on a cell phone or other device is acceptable in your state.

- **Check for Communication Barriers** Confirm that you and the signer can understand one another without outside help. California, for example, prohibits interpreters for notarial acts. Colorado, Arizona, and Montana allow them under specific conditions. Never assume your state follows another state's rules, verify your state's interpreter policies before accepting an appointment involving language barriers
- If there's a language barrier, consider referring to another mobile notary you know who can speak the language or to a Remote Online Notary (RON) in a state that allows the use of interpreters.

SUMMARY: ORIENTING THE SIGNER

You can make the notarization process smooth and confident by being prepared to guide your signer through the steps and knowing your alternate notarial options for signatures and ID. During this process, besides direct questions, observe and engage your signer to get an overall picture of how alert and aware they are before filling out your certificate. The integrity of this document relies on your professional assessment of the signer's capacity and consent. Aside from asking direct questions, you should observe and engage your signer to get an overall picture of their alertness and awareness. If you are confident in assessing your signer's orientation, you can observe and determine whether they're acting under coercion. If you know your alternate options for identification, the notarization process will go smoothly. The integrity of the document relies on your professional assessment of the signer's capacity and consent.

KEY TAKEAWAYS

→ Greet the signer warmly and explain your role.

→ Ask soft, non-invasive orientation questions: What is your name? Where are you today? What document are we signing? Do you want to sign it?

→ If the signer struggles, give them a chance to answer, but if they are unable to do so, ask the nursing staff whether any condition or medication may affect capacity.

→ Confirm acceptable ID or previously discussed credible witness plan.

→ Language barriers? In most states, to ensure direct communication, interpreters are not permitted.

→ If needed, explore alternatives of a Remote Online Notary (RON) in a state that allows interpreters.

CHAPTER 11

CONDUCTING THE SIGNING

Executing a notarization in a medical facility presents unique challenges that don't exist in typical mobile appointments. Limited space, medical equipment, interrupted signers, and family dynamics all require adaptation of your standard procedures. This chapter walks you through the actual signing process, from document review to certificate completion, with specific strategies for bedside conditions. Understanding these adaptations ensures legally compliant notarizations even in the most challenging environments.

The moment has arrived. But unlike typical signings, bedside notarizations often require creative solutions, more time, and a deeper level of patience. Once you've confirmed the signer is aware, willing, and able to proceed, it's time to complete the notarization.

In a hospital or skilled nursing environment, this process requires flexibility, attention to legal details, and a steady hand — literally and figuratively.

NOTARIZATION OF SIGNATURE:

Identify the notarial action you need to take either in the certificate language or in the instructions with phrases like:
- acknowledge the signature
- sign before a notary
- swear or take an oath before the notary

If it is compliant, meaning it meets your state laws fill it out and sign and stamp. If not, replace it with a "like" certificate. If there is not one, ask signer what type of notarization they need.

When no certificate is pre-printed or attached, the signer is responsible for choosing the appropriate one, such as an acknowledgment, jurat, or signature witnessing. Do not choose for them. Here is the language contained in each of them, followed by related questions:

- **Acknowledgment:** It must have the word "acknowledged" in it; if not, it may be another notarial act. This certificate certifies that you proved the principal signer who personally appeared and signed the document willingly is the one named in the document. They may have signed days or weeks ahead of time, so the date for their signature may be days or weeks before the current day. *Do you acknowledge that you willingly signed this document for its intended purpose?*
- **Jurat:** The notary must administer an oath or affirmation. "Subscribed and sworn before me" is a key phrase. You must watch them sign. These words mean they are signing under the penalty of perjury. Tell the signer that an oath or affirmation is required. Suggested Oath: *Do you solemnly swear or affirm that the contents of this document are true?*
- **Signature Witnessing: You witnessed the signature on the document.** You **will not see the word "acknowledged,"** and it may say "signed, sealed, and delivered" or "signed before me." Again, this proves who signed the document and on which day, since you watched it happened.

Speak clearly, and do not allow anyone else in the room to answer on the signer's behalf.

CONFIRM ID

At this stage, you should request the identification previously discussed during intake. Record the type of ID used and its expiration date. Now is not the time to discover that their ID is unavailable, as the appointment will have to be stopped unless credible witnesses are available. Make sure the ID meets your state's requirements.

VERIFY DOCUMENT READINESS

Check that the document is complete and free of blank spaces. Ensure the signer understands what they are signing and that it aligns with your earlier discussion.

ENSURE INDEPENDENT SIGNATURE

The signer must sign the document themselves, unless your state allows signature by mark or by proxy. Guide the signer through the actual signing of the document:

- If they struggle to hold a pen or a clipboard, **you or a family member may assist by holding the clipboard or placing the pen** in their hand, but **you cannot guide their hand** or make contact that would influence the motion of signing.
- Allow plenty of time. Fatigue, tremors, or unsteadiness are common. A shaky signature is still valid, if it is made willingly and independently.

If the signer's mark is inconsistent with their ID signature, document the circumstances in your journal.

Use Your Journal Strategically, this is your memory and can protect you later.

Even if your state does not require a notary journal, maintaining one is best practice, especially in hospital or hospice settings, where records may later be contested. If your state has requirements for journal entries, follow them if not record the following at minimum:

- Name of signer
- Type of notarial act performed
- Name of Document presented
- Date of signing
- Signature of signer
- Additional notes"
- Prescreening results
- Name of caller if not signer
- Any complications
- If signing was discontinued and why

- If you served as a witness (e.g., for a last will), document that too, including the names of any co-witnesses

If using an e-journal, follow the same guidelines and include digital notes where available

CONSIDER THE PHYSICAL ENVIRONMENT

Be prepared for small spaces, uncomfortable angles, or cluttered trays. If needed:
- Use your clipboard
- Provide signing pens (and extras for glove use)
- Carry pens with soft grips for signers with limited hand strength

Remain professional, calm, and unhurried. Your steady presence helps reassure the signer and the family.

KEY TAKEAWAYS

→ Double-check that the certificate complies with state law; if it is absent, ask the signer to specify which one they'd like to use.

→ Journal use is best practice—even in states that don't require it. Note anything unusual.

→ Record special circumstances: family interference, discontinuation, or acting as a will witness.

→ Allow breaks if the signer becomes fatigued.

→ Help position tools, such as a clipboard or a pen, but never guide the signer's hand.

Once you understand how to conduct the signing itself, you may wonder whether technology could simplify the process in medical settings. The next chapter examines electronic and remote notarization options and explains why traditional in-person methods remain the standard for bedside work.

CHAPTER 12

IN-PERSON ELECTRONIC NOTARIZATION AND REMOTE ONLINE NOTARIZATION (RON)

*When using technology makes
sense and when it doesn't*

Most bedside notarizations happen in person with paper documents—and for good reason. However, technology-based notarization options exist that may occasionally serve as alternatives when traditional methods aren't feasible. This chapter examines In-Person Electronic Notarization (IPEN) and Remote Online Notarization (RON) specifically through the lens of medical facility work.

Understanding these tools doesn't mean you'll use them regularly. In fact, the practical limitations of hospital environments—spotty Wi-Fi, heavily medicated signers, restricted document types, and difficulty assessing capacity remotely—make traditional notarization the better choice in most cases. But there are rare situations where technology might be appropriate: a tech-savvy, alert signer in medical isolation, or a family member who needs to participate remotely in a healthcare directive signing.

This chapter helps you evaluate when (and whether) these technological options make sense, understand their significant limitations in medical settings, and recognize when traditional in-person notarization remains the only viable option. Consider this your "know it exists, use it rarely" reference guide.

IPEN OVERVIEW

As of this printing, In-Person Electronic Notarization (IPEN) is allowed in 46 U.S. states; Alaska, Georgia, Hawaii, and Massachusetts do not permit it. During an IPEN, the document signer and notary meet in person, and the document is in an electronic format that gets signed and notarized using an electronic signature and seal.

The tools the notary uses include an IPEN system and an electronic seal. This option may work with signers who are more tech-savvy and less compromised.

Even with the ease of using IPEN, medical facilities may not always be the best place to use this technology. This is especially so in cases where the signer is contagious, and the equipment must be sanitized after touching. Also, connectivity can be an issue.

Remember, if your document is electronic, then the notary certificate must be as well. You cannot give a paper certificate to a signer for an electronic document, and a paper document cannot have an electronic signature; it must be original and manually affixed.

The upside of using IPEN:
- Most notary laws that apply to paper-based notarial acts apply to IPEN, and the notary should already be familiar with them. The rules for identifying a document signer, assessing signer competence and willingness to sign, completing a notarial certificate, and recording a journal entry, if required, are the same for traditional notarizations and IPEN. IPEN may work better if they only have an electronic version of their document that can be sent to the notary.

RON

To date, Remote Online Notarization (RON) is legal in 46 states and can be a viable alternative to in-person notarization. For bedside notaries, it may seem like an appealing option, especially when a patient or signer cannot have in-person visitors due to medical restrictions; however, RON has its own rules, limitations, and challenges that must be considered before you offer it as part of your service menu for medical facilities. Although I do not have direct experience with RON, as the approved law in California is not activated until 2030, I have interviewed RON notaries in other states about their experience, and they provided me with many insights about upsides and considerations for online sessions in medical facilities.

LICENSING AND PLATFORM REQUIREMENTS

In some states, performing RON requires an expanded notary commission or even a separate commission. In all cases, you must use a platform that supports real-time audio-video communication and meets one or the other conditions:

- It is on your state's approved vendor list, **or**
- It meets your state's technical requirements for RON.

These platforms are designed to capture and record the signing process through audio and visual means and store an audit trail securely, but they are not free. You'll incur platform costs—sometimes even if the notarization isn't complete.

WHEN RON MIGHT BE THE RIGHT CHOICE

RON can be suitable in certain circumstances:

- The signer is medically isolated, and no in-person visit is possible.
- The signer is alert, comfortable with technology, and has access to the required equipment (laptop, tablet or phone) and a **stable internet connection**.
- The document is legally permitted to be notarized electronically in your state.

PRACTICAL LIMITATIONS IN A HOSPITAL SETTING

While RON sounds flexible, bedside notaries know that hospital and care facility environments present specific challenges:

- **Technology access:** The signer must have their device and reliable internet. Hospital Wi-Fi is often spotty or blocked due to security concerns. This may prevent your connection or create "dropping" of internet service multiple times during the session.

- **ID verification:** Most platforms require at least two methods of verification:
- Credential analysis of a government-issued ID
- The notary must also review the ID onscreen.
- Knowledge-Based Authentication (KBA) questions or Biometric
- KBA may be more difficult than in other environments due to potential reduction in processing or memory due to medication or diagnosis.
- **Document restrictions** Pour-over or Last Wills:
- Some states, like **California, r**equire a "wet" signature for this document
- In **Colorado** the patient must be served by a Colorado online notary.
- In **Florida,** there is a restriction on the financial power of attorney.
- **Signer tech skills** If the signer struggles with using the device or platform, the notary often ends up in a "tech support" role, which can derail the appointment.
- **Advance document preparation:** The document must be uploaded and sent to the notary before the appointment. The signer may be limited in what they can do, especially if they do not have the ability to scan documents on their device.
- **Assessing willingness and capacity:** Reading body language, gauging alertness, and confirming willingness is more difficult through a screen.
- In Florida, there are extra online statutes for "vulnerable people," which is defined and requires more vetting of the patient/signer than others. And if the document requires witnesses, then they must appear in person.
- In North Carolina, they have required American with Disabilities Act (ADA) accommodations for their online platforms. These notaries should be aware of the possible accommodation for their signers.

IS RON A GOOD CHOICE FOR MEDICAL FACILITY CASES?

While RON can be the right solution for the right signer, it's often suboptimal in medical environments. The technology barriers, legal restrictions, and extra difficulty in assessing signer readiness make in-person notarization a better choice in most cases. If you do offer RON, be sure you know your own online rules and that you are asking the right questions. You should also be compensated for your time and platform expenses, even if the appointment doesn't go through.

Summary This chapter covers two electronic notarization options—**In-Person Electronic Notarization (IPEN)** and **Remote Online Notarization (RON)**—and evaluates their practical application for bedside notaries.

IPEN allows a signer and notary to meet face-to-face while completing an electronic document with electronic signatures and seals. Most rules for traditional notarization apply, making it familiar to experienced notaries. While IPEN can streamline document handling for tech-comfortable signers, hospital settings pose challenges, such as sanitizing equipment for contagious patients and dealing with inconsistent connectivity.

RON enables a notary to perform notarization entirely online, with the signer and notary in separate locations. It is legal in 45 states but may require additional licensing and approved platforms. RON can be useful when in-person visits aren't possible due to medical restrictions, but hospital conditions often limit its effectiveness. Issues include poor Wi-Fi, restricted document types, strict ID verification requirements, and difficulty assessing a signer's willingness or capacity remotely.

While both IPEN and RON have their place, bedside notaries must weigh legal requirements, technical feasibility, and the signer's comfort level. In most medical environments, traditional in-person notarization remains the most practical choice.

KEY TAKEAWAYS

→ **IPEN** keeps the signer and notary in the same room but uses electronic documents, signatures, and seals; familiar rules apply, but hospitals may pose sanitation and connectivity issues.

→ **RON** is fully remote, requiring state-approved platforms, strong internet, and a tech-capable signer; many hospital settings make this impractical.

→ Both methods have document restrictions; some forms, like wills, are often excluded from electronic notarization.

→ Assess each situation carefully; technology solutions are only practical when legal, logistically feasible, and comfortable for the signer.

WHEN IPEN WORKS BEST
- Signers are alert, willing, and tech-comfortable
- Internet connection is **stable**
- The environment is **low risk for contamination** (minimal sanitation concerns)
- The document is **already electronic** and permitted for electronic notarization in your state.
- Notary has **IPEN platform access** and an electronic seal ready

WHEN IPEN IS NOT IDEAL
- Signer is **contagious**, requiring equipment sanitation after each use
- **Hospital Wi-Fi** or device connection is unreliable
- Signers are confused, fatigued, or uncomfortable using technology
- Document type is **restricted** from electronic notarization by law
- Only a **paper copy** of the document exists

For most bedside notarizations, traditional in-person methods remain your best option.

Whether you've completed a traditional in-person notarization or used one of the technology alternatives discussed in this chapter, your professional responsibilities extend beyond the moment the signer puts down the pen. The steps you take after completing the notarization protect your practice, serve your client's ongoing needs, and build the foundation for future referrals.

CHAPTER 13

NAVIGATING CHALLENGES
WITH SIGNER

Interruptions, fatigue, and flexibility

Medical environments are inherently unpredictable, with interruptions, emergencies, and changing conditions that can disrupt even the best-planned appointments. Your ability to handle these challenges professionally while maintaining legal standards separates competent bedside notaries from those who struggle in this specialty. This chapter prepares you for the most common disruptions you'll face and provides strategies for managing them without compromising the notarization or your relationship with families and medical staff.

Your ability to maintain professionalism while upholding notarial standards is what will build your reputation and referrals.

HANDLE INTERRUPTIONS GRACEFULLY

Interruptions are inevitable in these environments, but the way you handle them makes all the difference.

Expect doctors, nurses, aides, or technicians to enter the room for vital signs, medication administration, or check-ins. Pause the signing respectfully and resume when appropriate. Remain patient and use the time to organize documents or quietly observe the signer's ongoing awareness.

WHEN MEDICAL STAFF ENTERS THE ROOM

Say: *I'll pause while you finish. Just let me know when I can continue.*

You may need to step out briefly or reposition to avoid being in the way of treatment.

WATCH FOR SIGNER FATIGUE DURING LONG APPOINTMENTS; KNOW WHEN TO PAUSE OR END

For signings with multiple documents, such as a living trust package, be alert for signs of exhaustion. Try this if the signer becomes too tired:
- Offer a short break so they can stretch, breathe, shift position, or have a sip of water (if permitted).
- Resume only when they're ready and are capable of continuing.
- If the signer becomes unresponsive, confused, or overwhelmed, it's okay to pause and reschedule. Your journal should reflect what occurred, who was present, and why you chose not to proceed.

RESPECT THE SIGNER'S PACE

A medical facility is not the place for speed notarization. Each bedside appointment needs ample time, not just for the signing itself, but to honor the human experience of the signer. Please give them your full presence. A rushed visit increases the chance for error, and it may make the signer or their family feel dismissed.

Hospital and hospice patients may move or speak slowly. Build in time for this. Rushing or pushing ahead could invalidate notarization or increase the risk of error.

You may be the last person to help them execute a vital document. Show up with calm professionalism and flexibility, and you will be remembered for the right reasons.

FAMILY DYNAMICS/FAMILY INTERFERENCE

It's common for family members to interject—sometimes with good intentions, sometimes with pressure. If a family member begins speaking for the signer, prompting answers, or rushing the signer, using calm but direct language:

I appreciate your help, but I need to speak directly with [signer's name] to ensure this is voluntary and clear. Remember, gently but firmly redirect attention back to the signer. Your job is to ensure that the signer is acting independently and willingly.

ENVIRONMENTAL DISRUPTIONS

Noisy roommates, hallway distractions, and meal delivery carts can interrupt the flow. When necessary, pause and re-establish a calm space before continuing. Ask staff if a quieter time is possible if the distractions persist.

MAINTAIN A CALM PRESENCE

Even if the family is upset or impatient, your professionalism and steadiness will set the tone. You are not there to fix the situation—only to ensure that legal requirements are met.

DOCUMENT ANY DEVIATIONS

If you encounter issues, such as having to pause for medical care or only completing part of the signing, please note them clearly in your journal.

KEY TAKEAWAYS

→ Expect and adapt to interruptions or changing conditions.
→ Watch for signer fatigue; pause or reschedule if needed.
→ Redirect family interference to focus on the signer's will.

→ Stay calm, professional, and flexible in all situations.

CHAPTER 14

TOOLS OF THE TRADE

What to keep in your notary bag

Standard notary supplies that work perfectly in offices and homes may be inadequate or inappropriate for medical facility environments. Bedside appointments require specialized tools that accommodate limited space, hygiene requirements, and signers with physical limitations. This chapter details the essential equipment for bedside work, from sanitizable clipboards to adaptive pens to emergency backup supplies. Being properly equipped demonstrates preparedness and ensures you can complete appointments regardless of the conditions you encounter.

1. NOTARY ESSENTIALS

Your core notary tools should always be present, functioning, and easy to access:

- **Notary stamp/seal,** with a backup if possible
- **Notary journal:** paper or digital, depending on your state
- **Acknowledgment, jurat and signature witnessing (if in your state) certificate forms:** with state-compliant wording, I have my certificates as stamps as well so if there is room, I can place the wording on the document rather than attaching.
- **Black and blue pens:** at least three to five of each
- **Thumbprint pad or e-device,** California specific (required documents include POAs and Real estate documents)

2. SIGNING SURFACE TOOLS

You can't rely on the facility to provide a workable surface. Be prepared to adapt with these tools:
- **Sturdy clipboard:** ideal for bedridden signers who can't sit up.
- **Slant boards or lap desks:** optional but helpful if you want to offer a more ergonomic surface.
- **Non-slip folder or portfolio** keeps papers flat when there's no table space.

 ✦ **PRO TIP:** Opt for a clipboard with a sturdy clip and a storage compartment for loose documents.

3. HYGIENE & SAFETY SUPPLIES

You must protect yourself, the signer, and your tools in medical environments:
- **Medical-grade masks,** in case the facility doesn't provide them or you're ill (cold or allergies)
- Hand sanitizer
- Disinfecting wipes or spray to clean your tools:
- Notary stamp
- Clipboard
- Journal cover
- Pens used by signers
- **Extra pens** to leave when needed

4. ACCESSIBILITY AIDS

Some patients may have limited motor skills or strength. These inexpensive tools can ease the process:
- Thick-barrel or easy-grip pens
- **Signature guides:** these are guides to help the signer stay on the line by having an opening in the middle of the guide
- **Magnifying lens** or reader glasses for patients with vision impairment

5. IDENTIFICATION AND VERIFICATION AIDS

- ID Reference Guide: It helps you verify acceptable IDs following your state's law
- **Credible witness guidelines:** quick checklist to explain requirements when ID is not available
- **Mini flashlight or phone light:** for dim rooms to examine ID properly
- Magnifying card: for small print

6. WITNESS RESOURCES

If your service includes locating witnesses (for a fee or courtesy):

- **Witness request forms:** quick agreement forms when you provide a disinterested witness
- **Contact list of local witnesses:** fellow notaries, colleagues, your friends, and family

7. BACKUPS & BUSINESS TOOLS

- **Power bank:** to charge your phone or tablet if you're using an e-journal
- **Mobile hotspot**: especially if you need to connect for online payments or scanning
- **Portable scanner app**: for assignments requiring immediate document return
- **Payment app access**: Zelle, PayPal, Square, Venmo, or whatever you use

8. EXTRAS THAT SHOW YOU CARE

Little touches that show empathy go a long way in hospital environments:

- Mini tissue packs
- **A small notepad for the signer** to jot down a reminder or a question for family
- Dollar Store reader glasses or a magnifier

Remember: The goal is to be self-contained and prepared for anything, but not to carry so much that it becomes burdensome.

SUMMARY: TOOLS OF THE TRADE

Hospital and care facility assignments often come with physical con-straints—tight rooms, low lighting, or fragile signers. Having the right tools and knowing how to use them with care and efficiency can make a significant difference in the notary's success and the signer's comfort.

KEY TAKEAWAYS

→ Use a lightweight clipboard that can be sanitized easily and is comfortable for bedbound signers.

→ Carry a variety of pens with easy-grip designs to accommodate shaky hands.

→ Bring an ID guide and notarial certificates to handle various sit-uations.

→ Use zip pouches or small bins to organize your supplies for quick access in tight spaces.

→ Always carry backup power or printed materials if relying on a mobile device for journaling or reference.

CHAPTER 15

DOCUMENT WITNESSES

Non-notarial witnesses

Many documents requiring bedside notarization may also need witness signatures, creating additional complexity in already challenging environments. Most medical facilities cannot provide witnesses, leaving families scrambling to meet legal requirements they may not understand. This chapter explains witness requirements, helps you guide families through the planning process, and outlines how to provide witness services when appropriate. Understanding witness protocols prevents appointment failures and positions you as a comprehensive solution provider.

Witness requirements are highly state-specific. Some states require witnesses for certain documents, others don't. Some allow notaries to serve as witnesses, others prohibit it. And some documents the preparer has set the document up to include witnesses even when not required by law. Always verify your state's rules before agreeing to provide or arrange witnesses.

1. UNDERSTAND WHICH DOCUMENTS REQUIRE WITNESSES

Not every document that you see will require a witness, but some **must** have one or more to be valid or have them built in, even if not required by law, examples include:
- Advance health care directives (can be notarized instead of 2 witnesses)
- Durable powers of attorney for health care
- Living trusts: pour over will, or other estate planning documents

- **Last will:** although not notarized, they are almost always double-witnessed

Always ask during intake:

Does the document require a witness—and how many? Have them check the document. Witness signature lines are usually placed after the principal's signature and before the notarial certificate.

Witness requirements should be based on the document instructions, or place for the witnesses to sign on the document or state law rather than on someone's assumption.

2. THE MEANING OF "DISINTERESTED"

Witnesses must be **disinterested parties**. This means:
- They are not named in the document as a party/signer.
- They are not family members or the spouse of the signer, when specific instructions are listed.
- They will not benefit financially or personally from the document.
- They are at least 18 years old (or per state requirement).
- They must show a valid ID if required by your state or document instructions.
- They are willing to sign and understand their role.
- For health care directives, witnesses cannot be health care providers.

> ✦ TIP : If a hospital staff member volunteers to be a witness, verify that it is not against facility policy. Confirm with them and your client that they are not related to or listed in the document.

3. ASSIST THE CALLER IN PLANNING AHEAD

Most hospitals and skilled nursing facilities do **not provide witnesses** as part of their patient services. It is essential to set that expectation when you take the initial call.

Offer the following guidance to the caller:

- Request that they identify two people in advance who they can bring who meet the criteria
- Tell the caller that witnesses may also need to bring a **valid ID**

If the signer cannot provide witnesses, you may assist:
- Offer to bring professional witnesses, for an additional fee
- **Reschedule** the appointment for a time when witnesses can be present
- In some cases, refer the caller to an **attorney** for directions to determine if witnesses are necessary for the execution of the document.

4. WITNESSING VS. NOTARIZING

When asked to serve as a witness in addition to notarizing, be cautious:
- Some states prohibit the notary from acting as **both** notary and witness on the **same** document
- Even where allowed, consider the **appearance of bias or conflict**
- If you agree to serve as a witness to a last will document, for example, **log this in your journal** ("Served as a witness only")

If you serve as **one** of two **required witnesses**, you'll need another disinterested party. Ensure your role is clear—either as **only the notary** or as **witness plus notary (when permitted).**

5. PREPARE YOUR WITNESSES

Remind the client or caller:
- Witnesses should **be present at the same time** as the signing, however for an acknowledgment, they signer could have signed ahead of time when the witnesses were there, but never after notarization
- They should arrive **promptly** to avoid delays
- Witnesses will likely be asked to:
- Sign on the witness line(s)
- Print their name and may include contact info
- Show ID if needed (some states or institutions request this)

Best practice: Bring extra pens and ensure witnesses have a clean surface on which to sign.

6. HOSPITAL-SPECIFIC CHALLENGES

Some medical facilities have added complications:
- **Limited visiting hours** may restrict when witnesses can enter
- **Sign-in procedures** may delay their arrival
- **Waiting areas** may be crowded or closed
- In some secure or ICU units, **only family** is allowed inside, so create a plan for this ahead of time.

Whenever possible, ask: *Have you gotten approval for the witnesses to be in the room with the notary at the same time?* Approval is essential, as many facilities do not allow more than two visitors at a time.

7. DOCUMENTATION AND PROFESSIONALISM

If you arrange to bring the witness(es):
- **Charge appropriately** since this is a separate service
- Unless you are using your spouse, be sure to pay your witnesses so they will help if asked again.
- **Get agreement** for payment from the client
- **Disclose witness names** in your journal notes, even if it is not required
- Keep good notes of what you did or did not do, as any signing may be challenged.

By anticipating witness needs and guiding your clients with clarity and care, you avoid unnecessary appointment delays and cancellations and prevent the submission of invalid documents.

OFFERING ADDITIONAL SERVICES

While the core function of the notary is to witness and affirm signatures, bedside signings sometimes call for extended services. When appropriate and within your scope, offering add-ons can meet client needs and increase your value. An example might be:
- printing services
- courier services
- scanning services

- recording services
- other non-related. (I shipped a set of keys to the spouse for a hospice patient.)

SUMMARY

Document witnesses are not notarial witnesses, and notaries would not know if witnesses are a requirement. Let the document or document holder tell you what is needed. If they choose not to use witnesses on a document with spaces for it, have them address the witness lines so they are not left blank.

KEY TAKEAWAYS

→ Notary witnesses may be offered as an added paid service when appropriate and allowed by law.

→ Consider bundling common services such as printing, delivery, or courier tasks.

→ Be transparent about pricing upfront, especially if additional witnesses or wait time are involved.

→ Stay within the scope of your role; refer to professionals for document drafting or legal guidance.

→ Make service enhancements part of your branding and marketing for bedside notarizations.

CHAPTER 16

AFTER THE APPOINTMENT

Follow-up and recordkeeping

Your professional responsibility doesn't end when you cap your pen. The steps you take immediately after a bedside notarization protect your business, support your signer's ongoing needs, and lay the groundwork for future referrals. This chapter covers essential post-appointment procedures, from secure documentation to appropriate follow-up communications. These final touches often determine whether families remember you as just another service provider or as a trusted professional they'll recommend to others.

1. OFFER CLOSURE TO THE SIGNER AND FAMILY

Before leaving the room:
- **Thank the signer** and reassure them that their documents are now completed as requested.
- **Let the family or the caller know** what happened, especially if they are paying you or coordinating delivery.
- **Answer any remaining questions and** be careful not to give legal advice. Refer them to the attorney who may have prepared the documents if legal concerns arise.
- **Hand out business cards** to the staff or witnesses for future referrals.

2. CONFIRM PAYMENT AND RECEIPT OPTIONS

Make sure to complete all payment details:

- If you collect payment in person, **issue a paper or electronic receipt**.
- If payment is still due, remind them of the agreed method (cash, card, Zelle, PayPal, etc.) and due date.
- **Document any unpaid fees** and follow up promptly if necessary.

If you agreed to deliver or mail documents:
- Confirm the recipient's name and address or email if scanning.
- Offer tracking or delivery confirmation, where applicable.

3. SECURE YOUR JOURNAL AND TOOLS

After the appointment:
- Double-check your notary journal or e-journal for complete and accurate entries.
- **Note any unusual circumstances, such as** family interference, need to pause, or multiple attempts at signing.
- If you served as a witness for a will, as an example, enter that in your notes section.
- Sanitize any tools used, including your journal cover, clipboard, and notary stamp.

Store your journal and stamp securely, especially if your next stop is another appointment.

4. FOLLOW UP WHEN APPROPRIATE

A professional follow-up builds trust and reminds the customer that they made the right choice in selecting the notary.

Examples of thoughtful follow-ups:
- A **thank you text or email** to the person who arranged the appointment
- **Confirmation** of when the notarized documents were mailed, delivered, or scanned
- For ongoing relationships with staff (e.g., hospital social workers or case managers), a **friendly check-in** a week later can encourage referrals.

✦ **TIP:** Keep a contact log of the people who referred to you and the facilities you served. Over time, this becomes a gold mine of repeat clients and opportunities for relationship building.

5. REFLECT AND IMPROVE

Bedside notarizations often vary widely in environment, signer condition, and staff cooperation. After each one, take a moment to reflect on these areas:

- What went well?
- What can I improve upon?
- Are there any additional supplies I should include in my notary bag?
- Was my intake process thorough enough to avoid surprises? How can I revise my intake form to be better prepared next time?

These reflections help refine your process and ensure that you consistently deliver high-quality service.

HANDLING EMOTIONAL SITUATIONS

Hospital signings often occur during life's most challenging chapters. Emotions may run high, and your presence as a calm, nonjudgmental professional can provide reassurance. Navigating emotional terrain requires sensitivity, empathy, and clear boundaries.

KEY TAKEAWAYS

→ Acknowledge emotions but remain professionally neutral—your calm presence matters.

→ Be prepared for last-minute changes, breakdowns, or shifts in family dynamics.

→ Don't rush the process, even when the room feels tense—protect the signer's clarity and consent.

→ Avoid providing legal or medical commentary, and redirect questions as needed.

→ Your compassion can be communicated through tone, patience, and presence, more than words.

CHAPTER 17

BEHAVIORAL & PSYCHIATRIC FACILITIES

Special considerations

Behavioral health and psychiatric facilities present unique challenges that go beyond typical hospital protocols. Patients in these settings may face blanket capacity assumptions, restricted visitor access, and complex legal questions about their ability to sign documents. This chapter prepares you for the specialized considerations of mental health facilities, where institutional policies and patient conditions require extra caution and thorough documentation. Understanding these distinctions helps you navigate the delicate balance between serving patients' legal needs and respecting facility safeguards designed to protect vulnerable individuals.

These environments have strict protocols and heightened privacy regulations that impact notarial access and the signer's eligibility.

ACCESS MAY BE RESTRICTED

These facilities may be **locked units** or require **special clearance** for outside visitors, including notaries.

Not all patients are allowed outside visitors--even family members--so always verify access ahead of time.

Be prepared for stricter security protocols than those typically found in general hospitals.

CAPACITY ASSUMPTIONS VARY BY FACILITY

Many facilities adopt a **blanket policy** that assumes all patients are temporarily unable to sign legal documents.

These policies may be **overly cautious**, but legally, a notary cannot override them.

Some facilities **require a doctor's written clearance** before allowing notarizations to take place.

Best Practice: When a family member calls, ask: *Has the attending physician cleared your loved one to sign legal documents?* And then confirm with the unit in advance.

SIGNER MUST STILL BE PRESCREENED

Even with clearance, the notary must independently assess alertness, awareness, and willingness.

Behavioral health patients may have lucid intervals, **"clear windows"**—where they are capable of understanding and consenting.

These windows may be brief, so timing and flexibility are crucial.

DOCUMENT TYPES OFTEN REQUESTED
- Power of attorney—often financial or health care
- Advanced Health Care Directive
- Revocation of a previous POA
- Release forms or applications for guardianship/conservatorship

Red Flag: Family members may urgently request that these documents be signed in an attempt to gain control over a patient's finances or medical choices. Proceed with **extreme caution** and maintain signer-focused ethics.

OTHER CONSIDERATIONS

- Confirm **witness needs.** Staff will rarely serve as witnesses.
- Some facilities have a **case worker** who may help you coordinate timing or assess capacity.
- Notaries should document all prescreening conversations in their journal, especially if they later decline to proceed.

KEY TAKEAWAYS FOR BEHAVIORAL FACILITIES

→ It is a good idea to confirm whether a medical professional has cleared the signer to execute legal documents.

→ Do not proceed if the facility policy prohibits signing, regardless of your assessment.

→ Assess alertness, awareness, and willingness, as usual. Clearance doesn't override notarial duty.

→ Maintain extra caution when families are involved in high-emotion or high-stakes signings.

→ Treat refusals to proceed as a **valid outcome**; protect yourself and the signer.

CHAPTER 18

HOSPICE ASSIGNMENTS

Special considerations

Hospice notarizations represent the most emotionally demanding and legally risky appointments you'll encounter as a bedside notary. During final weeks of life, patients are often heavily medicated, drifting in and out of consciousness, and facing imminent end-of-life decisions. Family pressure can be intense, and the window for valid notarization may be extremely narrow or already closed. This chapter addresses the special considerations of hospice work, helping you balance compassion with legal standards while protecting both the dying patient and you from failed or contested notarizations.

Notarizations in hospice facilities require not only professionalism but also exceptional emotional and ethical sensitivity.

HIGHER RISK OF INCOMPLETION

Patients in hospice care are frequently under strong medication, and they may drift in and out of consciousness. Due to this, these appointments carry the highest risk of being canceled or cut short because of a lack of alertness or awareness at the time of signing. I include it here as these can be fulfilling assignments.

I chose to volunteer for Hospice in my community, and I've found that families don't forget who helped their loved ones when they needed it most. They've even called me back for paid work later.

PRESCREEN THOROUGHLY

Have a detailed conversation with the family member or coordinator before accepting the job. Ask direct but compassionate questions to assess whether the signer is:

- Currently alert and oriented
- Awake consistently throughout the day
- Capable of communicating directly
- Able to hold a pen and sign, or use an allowed alternative

Suppose the answers are uncertain or vague, pause before proceeding. Ask more questions. Is this a time-of-day issue? Do they need accommodation? You may still be able to assist once you get more information.

EMOTIONAL APPEALS MAY ARISE

Family members may emphasize the importance of the document and ask you to "just get it done." In emotionally charged moments, it's not uncommon to feel pressure to proceed.

Remember: *You are the notary in the chair.* It's your responsibility to uphold the integrity of the process.

STICK TO THE STANDARDS

- Don't rely solely on a nurse, social worker, or family member's word.
- Trust your professional instincts—if something feels off, it probably is.
- Know what accommodations (e.g., signature by mark, communication aids) are allowed in your state.
- Document everything in your journal, especially if you decline to proceed.

KEY TAKEAWAYS FOR HOSPICE VISITS

→ Use soft orientation questions to assess awareness: Where are you today? What is your full name? What kind of document are we signing?

→ If the signer appears confused or struggles to respond, consult with the nursing staff to determine if medications, treatment, or conditions might impair their ability to sign.

→ Confirm the signer has a valid ID (or credible witnesses) as previously discussed during intake, and that it meets your state's requirements.

→ Verify that you and the signer can communicate clearly in the same language, without the aid of others, unless you are in a state that permits interpreters.

→ Watch for signs of **coercion**—including fear, hesitation, or the presence of dominating third parties. Always speak with the signer privately if you have concerns.

→ To assess willingness, ask open-ended questions, such as Do you know what power this document has? Or do you want to sign this document?

→ **Do not proceed** if you suspect the signer is being pressured or does not fully understand the document.

→ Document anything unusual in your journal, including signs of coercion or the reason for refusal, if applicable.

→ Be aware of your state's rules regarding signer awareness and voluntary participation. Some states, like Montana, have stronger language that includes competency.

→ Your professional integrity requires you to walk away if you're in doubt about the signer's willingness or awareness.

CHAPTER 19

FINAL TOUCHES

Building a reputable bedside notary brand

Your reputation as a bedside notary is built through every interaction, from the first phone call to your post-appointment follow-up. In medical facility work, where emotions run high and stakes are significant, the impression you leave determines whether families recommend you, facilities trust you, and referral sources remember you. This chapter shows you how to create a professional brand that reflects competence, compassion, and reliability. These relationship-building strategies transform one-time appointments into ongoing referral networks that sustain a thriving bedside notary practice.

This chapter focuses on how to build and maintain a brand identity that reflects the highest standards in medical facility bedside notarization.

1. YOUR BRAND IS BUILT BY EVERY INTERACTION

From the first phone call to the moment you leave the room, you are shaping someone's opinion about your service. Consistency in tone, patience, and preparation makes all the difference. Remember the 4 Ps:
- Be **punctual** – A late notary can cause stress. Communicate beforehand if you must be late.
- Be **presentable** – Dress with professionalism and wear your name badge.
- Be **prepared** – Carry the right supplies every time (clipboards, pens, spare certificate wording, PPE, etc.).
- Be **patient** – Signers may need extra time. Allow for it.

> ✦ **TIP:** Remember that the signer may not recall your name, but they'll remember how you made them feel.

2. LEAVE A POSITIVE, LASTING IMPRESSION

Going the extra mile doesn't require grand gestures; it just requires thoughtful ones. These touches make you memorable and appreciated.
- Offer a **business card** or small printed flyer to leave behind.
- Consider a **small "care" card** for the patient if appropriate (something uplifting but simple).
- Thank the staff if they helped facilitate the appointment.

3. STAY ORGANIZED AND PROFESSIONAL ON THE BACK END

Being reputable includes:
- **Invoicing promptly** when billing facilities or attorneys.
- Keep clear **records,** even if you're not required to.
- Send a **thank you or confirmation text** after a successful signing.
- Handle disputes or confusion with **grace and clarity.**

4. SOLICIT AND EARN REFERRALS THOUGHTFULLY

Hospitals, care managers, elder law attorneys, and hospice organizations are constantly seeking trusted notaries. Once you've established yourself, don't hesitate to:
- **Ask for referrals** with humility: If you ever need another notarization, I'd love to help.
- **Join local professional networks** that specialize in working with aging populations.
- Leave a few cards at the facilities, nurses' stations are a good place, where you've served and been well received.
- Ask for reviews for successful assignments; always judge if the situation is appropriate.

✦ **TIP:** Be mindful and never market during an appointment or push your services.

5. BUILD YOUR ONLINE PRESENCE

Even if most jobs come from word of mouth, your online presence validates your professionalism.
- Create your free Google Business Profile and optimize it.
- Maintain a clean, mobile-friendly website or landing page.
- Request reviews and, with permission, include testimonials from satisfied clients.
- Include a section describing your hospital **bedside notary services** with a reassuring tone.
- Ensure contact info is up-to-date and easy to find.

You may also consider:
- Listing yourself on senior care directories
- Joining the local chamber of commerce
- Writing blog posts or short educational articles about notarizing in medical environments
- Attending administrator or social worker networking groups
- Connecting with your local ombudsperson office
- Creating a program that educates medical staff who may coordinate securing a notary

✦ **TIP:** I highly recommend "On the Move, *The Relationship-Driven 5 Point Marketing System for Mobile Business Success*", authored by Jennifer Neitzel, for an organized path to marketing your services.

6. STAY CURRENT AND COMMITTED

The best bedside notaries are continually improving by deliberate practice:
- They keep up with state laws and certificate wording requirements
- They refresh their training regularly
- They attend relevant webinars and read articles about elder care, aging, and notary best practices.

- They update their intake procedures as new information becomes available.

You're not just filling out forms; you're building trust and serving families during their most vulnerable moments. Continue to sharpen your skills and adjust your approach with compassion and professionalism.

SUMMARY

In this chapter, I emphasize that a reputable bedside notary brand is built through professionalism, empathy, and consistent service from start to finish. Every interaction, from the first phone call to post-appointment follow-up, shapes your reputation and increases the likelihood of repeat work and referrals. Building trust with patients, families, and facility staff requires attention to appearance, punctuality, preparedness, and patience. The chapter also covers strategies for leaving a positive impression, maintaining organized business practices, respectfully requesting referrals, establishing a strong online presence, and staying current with laws and best practices to ensure long-term success.

KEY TAKEAWAYS

→ **Consistency builds trust:** Every touchpoint matters; be punctual, presentable, prepared, and patient.

→ **Small, thoughtful gestures leave a significant impact:** Business cards, thank-you cards, and kindness to staff create lasting goodwill.

→ **Professional systems matter:** Timely invoicing, precise record-keeping, and graceful dispute resolution reinforce credibility.

→ **Referrals and visibility fuel growth:** Ask for recommendations appropriately, maintain an online presence, and connect with local networks.

→ **Commit to continual improvement**: Stay current on laws, refresh your training, and adapt your approach with compassion.

CHAPTER 20

PRICING STRATEGIES

Charging for the value you bring

Many notaries undercharge for facility bedside work because they fail to account for the true complexity and value of medical facility appointments. Between facility navigation, unpredictable delays, emotional demands, and specialized knowledge required, these assignments deserve premium pricing. This chapter helps you develop a pricing structure that reflects the unique challenges of bedside notarization while remaining compliant with state fee regulations. Charging appropriately isn't just about profitability; it's about valuing your expertise and ensuring your bedside practice remains sustainable long-term. So why do many notaries hesitate when it comes to setting prices? The answer usually lies in mindset.

NEW MINDSET: VALUE OVER HOURLY RATES

Before we discuss numbers, let's address our beliefs.
- You're not "just a notary."
- You provide a **critical service** that people need to move forward with legal, financial, and personal matters, especially during vulnerable moments.
- Your role often determines whether a document is accepted or rejected by the agency that requested it, whether for adoption, medical authorization, international travel, or property transfer.
- You provide **access and outcomes, which are valuable!** Your pricing should reflect the unique challenges and value of what you deliver. (e.g., notarizing an advanced health care directive or power of attorney that allowed urgent decisions to be made)

KNOW YOUR STATE'S RULES

Always follow your state's laws regarding notary fees. Some states, such as California and Florida, permit additional unrestricted travel and convenience fees, provided they obtain agreement with the hiring party beforehand. Others, like North Carolina, Maryland, and Connecticut, who have tight regulations around travel, make profitability more challenging.

If you're in a restrictive state with a non-friendly travel fee policy, offering this service may be your **way to give back** rather than earn a profit. That's perfectly valid; be intentional in your pricing model. S**et boundaries** for pro bono work so it's sustainable.

PRICING REALISTICALLY FOR FACILITY WORK

Bedside appointments aren't the same as signing a document at a kitchen table. Consider what you might encounter:
- **Paid parking** blocks from the building
- **Security check-ins, metal detectors, bag inspections, time delays** due to elevators, directions, and the hospital layout all equate to MORE TIME.
- Medical interruptions, slow signers, or unexpected family involvement
- Alternative signing or ID verification methods
- **Garbing up** with gloves, a mask, and a cover for contagious patients

These all add up to a more time-consuming and stressful appointment.

> ✦ **TIP:** I recommend creating a "facility fee" that is added to your standard travel fee. This fee accounts for the extra time, effort, and unpredictability tied to these appointments.

BUNDLED FEES

If you're offering additional services, such as printing, acting as a witness, or delivering documents, consider offering a bundled fee that reflects the full scope of your effort, rather than charging each service separately. Clients prefer knowing the full cost upfront, which helps ensure that your time is covered. **Bundling benefits both sides**: for the notary (simplifies quoting, ensures profitability) and the client (clear, all-inclusive pricing).

SUMMARY

Shift your mindset to charge what your bedside notary services are worth confidently. It emphasizes valuing the unique access, outcomes, and compassion you provide. Understanding and complying with state laws and accounting for the extra time and logistical challenges of facility work is vital to a profitable and complaint business.

KEY TAKEAWAYS

→ Adopt a mindset that reflects the **value** of your work, not just the time it takes.

→ Know your **state's fee laws** and what's permitted for travel, service, and add-ons.

→ Charge more for medical facility visits—consider adding a facility fee on top of your regular travel costs.

→ Bundle your pricing when services go beyond notarization.

→ Profit is not a dirty word; you run a **business**, not a charity.

→ Giving away this service can be the right thing if you choose, but it is not a business model.

PART II:
QUICK REFERENCE TOOLS

The following section provides at-a-glance resources designed for quick consultation before, during, or after bedside appointments. While these concepts are explained in detail within the chapters, these condensed formats allow you to refresh your knowledge quickly or verify procedures on-site.

SAMPLE IN-TAKE FORM

Medical facility bedside notary appointment

Being expert at asking the caller the right questions will save you time and prevent you from travelling to appointments that cannot be fulfilled. You may use this as a printable sheet or digital intake form.

CALLER INFORMATION

NAME	RELATIONSHIP TO SIGNER

PHONE NUMBER	EMAIL
☐ Textable	

SIGNER INFORMATION

FULL NAME

FACILITY NAME	ROOM NUMBER

TYPE OF FACILITY
☐ Hospital   ☐ Skilled Nursing   ☐ Specialty Care

QUESTION	YES	NO	UNSURE
Is the signer alert and aware (per callers' observation)?	☐	☐	☐
Can the signer speak and understand English (or your language)?	☐	☐	☐

QUESTION	YES	NO	UNSURE
Can the signer sign their name without assistance?	☐	☐	☐
Does the signer have a government-issued ID that meets state requirements?	☐	☐	☐
If **not**, is there a plan to use credible witnesses?	☐	☐	☐

DOCUMENT INFORMATION

TYPE OF DOCUMENT(S):

QUESTION	YES	NO
Are witnesses required?	☐	☐
The caller/signer will provide disinterested witnesses	☐	☐
Requesting notary to bring a paid witness(es)	☐	☐
Will you email or text the document or signature page ahead of time?	☐	☐

SCHEDULING DETAILS

PREFERRED DATE/TIME:

FACILITY CONSIDERATIONS (shift change, mealtimes, medication schedule)*

If signer is taking any medication that can affect their ability to answer questions or sign name, then plan for as far after last dose, before the next one

SPECIAL INSTRUCTIONS (for parking, entrance, or contact upon arrival?)

FEE ACKNOWLEDGEMENT

QUOTED TRAVEL/SERVICE FEE:	QUOTED PER-SIGNATURE OR DOCUMENT FEE (IF APPLICABLE):

ACCEPTED PAYMENT METHODS:

☐ Cash   ☐ Credit Card   ☐ Zelle   ☐ Venmo   ☐ Other

Note: *If notarization cannot be completed due to the signer's incapacity or lack of identification, the travel fee may still apply. This is a business decision for you to make.*

CALLER AGREES TO THE TERMS AND FEE POLICY.
☐ Yes ☐ No

SAMPLE SIGNER
ASSESSMENT PROMPTS

I have put this separate from the chapter you would have read it in early, so that it is easy to access when you need it.

SAMPLE PROMPTS FOR SIGNER ORIENTATION
- Your name is?
- And where are you today?
- Do you know what this document is for, or can you describe what it is?
- Are you willing to sign it?
- Can you point/name the person listed as your agent (IF POA/AHCD)?

These questions help establish willingness, awareness, and independence.

QUICK HYGIENE CHECKLIST

Before and after each appointment

Item	Before	After
Hand sanitizer used	☐	☐
Clipboard wiped down	☐	☐
Stamp wiped down	☐	☐
Journal or device sanitized	☐	☐
Pens cleaned and set aside	☐	☐ *or discarded if used in PPE*
PPE, if required	☐	☐ *Appropriately discarded in the designated bin*

RON DECISION GUIDE FOR BEDSIDE NOTARIES

Here is a decision chart to help you decide if using this technology is appropriate for you.

Question	No	Yes
1. Is RON legal in your state?	Stop — must be in-person	Proceed to Q2
2. Do you have the required RON commission and/or approved platform?	Apply/obtain before offering RON	Proceed to Q3
3. Does the signer have their device (laptop/tablet) with a camera?	Recommend in-person notarization	Proceed to Q4
4. Is internet connection stable?	Recommend in-person notarization	Proceed to Q5
5. Is the signer alert, willing, and comfortable using technology?	Recommend in-person notarization	Proceed to Q6

Question	No	Yes
6. Is the document eligible for electronic notarization in your state?	Recommend in-person notarization	Proceed to Q7
7. Are you comfortable that ID verification (credential analysis + KBA) will be successful?	Recommend in-person notarization	Proceed with RON

RED FLAGS

Red Flag	What it Might Mean	Your Action
A family member answers on behalf of the signer.	*Possible coercion or incapacity*	Ask to speak with the signer alone and assess directly
Signer looks to others before answering.	*Pressure, or confusion*	Ask orientation questions privately to confirm willingness
No ID and no plan for credible witnesses.	*Unable to verify identity*	Do not proceed unless an alternate method is permitted
The document is incomplete or blank.	*Potential unauthorized or fraudulent use*	Do not notarize until the document is complete prepared
Signer is visibly drowsy, disoriented, or incoherent.	*Lack of awareness or capacity*	Pause, reassess, and document your observations

Red Flag	What it Might Mean	Your Action
Language barrier prevents communication.	*Cannot verify understanding or willingness*	Decline unless direct communication is possible or state allowance
Staff or the facility prohibits signing.	*Facility policy override*	Respect policy; do not force the appointment
The patient has recently received medication.	*Possible altered mental state*	Ask the staff about timing, or reschedule for later clarity
Signer is unable to sign, and alternatives are not legal in your state.	*Lack of physical ability to complete the signing*	Do not proceed unless proxy or mark is legally permitted

ADA QUICK REFERENCE GUIDE FOR NOTARIES

*Serving signers with confidence,
competence, and compassion*

The **Americans with Disabilities Act (ADA)** ensures equal access for individuals with disabilities. ADA requirements apply federally, but state notary laws govern how accommodations are implemented. Signature by mark is allowed in most states; signature by proxy is permitted in fewer states. Always confirm your state allows the accommodation method before using it.

As a notary, you are responsible for making **reasonable accommodations** while staying compliant with **state laws** and maintaining **impartiality**.

I. KEY PRINCIPLES FOR NOTARIES

What it means to provide equal service: Never refuse service solely because a signer has a disability.

Reasonable accommodations: Provide support—interpreters, assistive tools, or alternative signatures—without compromising legal requirements.

Stay neutral: Do not provide legal advice or interpret documents. Confirm identity, willingness, and awareness only.

2. COMMON ADA SCENARIOS FOR NOTARIES

Scenario	Best Practices
Signer Cannot Write	Use **signature by mark** or, if needed **signature by proxy**.
Signer Is Deaf / Hard of Hearing	Use written notes, tablets, or interpreters. Always confirm willingness directly with the signer.
Signer Is Blind / Visually Impaired	Confirm nature of documents verbally as well as understanding first. If needed, offer a trusted reader to go over the document, or to read significant parts such as proxy or agent, Dollar or percentage amounts. Use assistive tech if they have it. A signer's card for the visually impaired is helpful. A few states my have notary rules that require the document to be read out loud verbatim, for example Florida.
Signer Has Speech Impairment	Use yes/no questions, gestures, or written notes to confirm willingness and awareness.
Signer Has Cognitive Challenges	If the signer cannot communicate to notary satisfaction, about willingness or does not understand the document to be signed, **stop the notarization**.

3. SIGNATURE OPTIONS

A. *Signature by Mark* *(Allowed in most states)*
When a signer cannot produce a traditional signature:
- The signer makes a mark ("X" or other symbol) **in your presence**.
- Typically, two **neutral witnesses** observe the mark being made, and they sign both the document and your journal.
- Document all details thoroughly.

  ✦ **Pro Tip:** Always confirm your state's rules before proceeding; state requirements may vary.

B. *Signature by Proxy / Third Party* *(Allowed in some states)*
When the signer cannot make a mark:
- A neutral third party (not the notary) signs the document at the signer's direction.
- Both the signer and third party must be **present**.
- Modify the notarial certificate to include this: *"Signature affixed by [Name of Third Party] at the direction of [Signer's Name]."*
- Record full details in your journal.

  ✦ **Pro Tip:** Check your state's laws before using this method, as it isn't universally allowed.

4. BEST PRACTICES TO PROTECT YOURSELF AND THE SIGNER

- **Journal everything is written: Record** accommodations, witness names, and any deviations from a standard process.
- **Confirm willingness directly:** Even with interpreters or proxies, verify intent directly with the signer.
- **Watch for undue influence:** Ensure no one pressures or speaks for the signer.
- **Follow ID rules:** Disabilities don't change identification requirements.
- **Stay compassionate:** Approach every signing with patience.

KEY TAKEAWAYS

→ Serve **all signers equally.** Disabilities are never grounds for refusal.

→ Know your **signature alternatives** and state-specific requirements.

→ Stay **impartial.** Facilitate the process; don't interpret or advise.

→ **Document everything.** Your journal is your best protection.

OMBUDSMAN PROGRAM

Every state has a Long-Term Care Ombudsman Program thanks to a federal law called the Older Americans Act. The goal of this program is to protect and advocate for people living in long-term care settings like nursing homes, assisted living, and board-and-care homes. California requires an Ombudsman when an Advanced Health Care Directive is notarized in a long-term skilled nursing facility (Probate Code § 4701) . Should you see abuse when working in a long-term care facility, including assisted living (RCFE) this is the right organization to report it to whether you are considered a mandated reporter.

Each state has a lead Ombudsman who oversees the program and works with trained staff and volunteers who visit these facilities and speak on behalf of residents.

WHAT DOES THE OMBUDSMAN PROGRAM DO?

The program is there to help residents of care facilities live with dignity and receive quality care. Ombudsmen (and the volunteers they train) work directly with residents to solve problems, from complaints about care to concerns about rights and safety.

They provide these services:
- Educate residents, families, and staff about residents' rights and what constitutes good care.
- Make sure residents can reach an ombudsman when they need to.
- Support residents and family councils in the facilities.

- Speak up for better care and living conditions—locally and even nationally.
- Share information with the public about long-term care, resident rights, and policy changes.
- Representing residents when dealing with government agencies.
- Help find legal or other solutions when residents are at risk.

WHAT THEY DON'T DO:

It's important to know that Ombudsmen are not regulators or direct caregivers. They **do not provide these services:**
- Perform state inspections of care facilities,
- Handle Adult Protective Services (APS) investigations, or
- Provide medical or personal care.

SAMPLE PRICING SHEET

SAMPLE PRICING WORKSHEET FOR BEDSIDE NOTARY SERVICES

This worksheet helps you plan a pricing strategy that reflects your time, effort, and the unique demands of medical facility assignments. Adjust amounts according to your state regulations and business objectives.

- You can request payment in advance and then adjust it based on the actual work performed.
- You can request payment at the time of service, unless otherwise arranged.
- Have multiple payment options available like Zelle, Venmo, credit card, check, and cash.
- For longer travel distances, confirm that everything is ready and the signer is okay just before you leave.

Be sure to quote a trip fee that is due even if notarization is not completed, if that is your business plan. It is not required, and you may choose not to do so; that is okay. Some notaries collect this fee upfront before travel, some at the hospital but before notarization, and some at the completion.

FEE BUILDER

1. Notarization Fee (per signature)
Amount by State: $_____$
Number of Signatures Expected: _____
SUBTOTAL: $_____$

Note: If your state strictly regulates fees, skip the travel and service-based options.

2. Travel Fee
Base Travel Fee (within 10 miles): $_____
Additional Miles (x $_____/mile): $_____
TRAVEL FEE TOTAL: $_____

3. Facility Surcharge
For hospital/skilled nursing navigation, parking, wait time, security, etc.
Recommended: $25–$50 Facility Surcharge: $_____

4. Additional Services (Optional)
Add-On Services Subtotal: $_____

5. Estimated Total Quote
Notarization Fee: $_____
Travel Fee: $_____
Facility Surcharge: $_____
Add-Ons: $_____
GRAND TOTAL QUOTE: $_____

GLOSSARY

Vocabulary is especially important and elevates you immediately starting with taking the call. Presenting yourself as someone who is knowledgeable about your job, and the environment you work in will give the caller/family/signer confidence they have called the right person.

GLOSSARY OF MEDICAL AND NOTARIAL TERMS (ALPHABETICAL)

Acknowledgment: A notarial act in which the signer confirms that they voluntarily signed the document. ID is required; personal appearance is mandatory.

Acute Care: Short-term treatment for severe injuries or illnesses in hospitals with a focus on stabilization.

Advance Health Care Directive (AHCD): A legal document that combines a living will and medical power of attorney.

Affirmation: Like an oath, but without any religious reference, still a legally binding promise that what you say or sign is true.

Agent (in Power of Attorney): The person chosen to make decisions on behalf of someone else (the principal) in a legal document, like a POA.

Assisted Living Facility / Residential Care Home: Non-medical facilities that provide long-term help with daily living skills.

Charge Nurse: The lead nurse on duty for a specific hospital unit.

Credible Witness: A person who can swear to the identity of a signer when no ID is available. A credible witness does not benefit from the documents and may not act as a signer in the transaction.

Document Witness: An individual who is required to observe and typically sign a legal document. And in some cases, they provide contact information like a mailing address.

Disinterested Party: Someone who is not involved in the transaction and doesn't benefit from it. Often used as a neutral witness.

Do Not Resuscitate (DNR): A medical order stating that a patient does not want CPR or life-saving intervention.

Durable Power of Attorney: A power of attorney that remains valid even if the signer becomes mentally incapacitated.

Grant Deed / Quitclaim Deed: Legal instruments used to transfer real estate ownership. This document is recorded as public record upon notarization.

Health Proxy / Health Agent: The person appointed to make health decisions on behalf of the patient.

Hospital: A full-service facility for diagnosis, treatment, and acute care.

Hospice: A service and or care setting for terminally ill patients focusing on palliative care (comfort) rather than cure.

Jurat: A notarial act where the signer swears to or affirms the truth of a document in the notary's presence.

Testament: A legal document outlining posthumous (after death) asset distribution.

Living Trust: A legal arrangement managing assets during life, naming successor trustees in case of incapacitation, and distributing them after death.

Living Will: A document describing medical treatment preferences if the signer becomes unable to communicate.

Long-Term Care: for people who need assistance with daily living activities over an extended period.

MOLST / POLST: Physician orders for life-sustaining treatment used in end-of-life planning.

Notarial Certificate: The section of a document where the notary records the notarial act. Typically found after the signature line.

Oath: A spoken promise that what you say, or sign is true, made while calling on a higher power or personal belief system.

Ombudsman: A patient advocate who investigates complaints within long-term care facilities. This person is utilized in some states to confirm wishes for a living will or an advanced health care directive.

Power of Attorney (POA): Authorizes someone to act on another's behalf in legal, financial matters, and personal affairs.

Principal (in Power of Attorney): The person who creates and signs the document and who permits someone else to act on their behalf.

Rehabilitation Facility (Rehab): Provides therapy services, such as physical or speech rehabilitation.

Signature by Mark: An alternative signature for those unable to sign their regular signature, often just an "X," but not limited to that. It can be any mark the signer can produce.

Signature by Proxy: Allowed in some states, a proxy signs on behalf of the signer under their direction.

Signature Witnessing: A notarial act that proves the date of signing

Skilled Nursing Facility (SNF): Provides medical and therapeutic care under the supervision of licensed professionals. May include a rehabilitation section in the same building.

Social Services Department: The hospital unit helps patients transition post-care and connect with resources.

Specialty Hospital: A facility treating specific long-term conditions requiring medical interventions such as ventilators for respiratory, renal, and cardiac support, and stroke recovery

Transfer on Death Deed (TOD Deed): Transfers property directly to a beneficiary upon death, avoiding probate. Not in all states.

ACKNOWLEDGMENTS
& GRATITUDE

My deepest thanks to the healthcare professionals and families who have opened their hearts and shared their trust during bedside notarizations. Your resilience, grace, and care in the most challenging moments inspire every page of this work. To the notary community—your dedication to service and continuous learning is the heartbeat of why this book exists. You are the reason I do what I do.

I am blessed beyond measure by my inner circle of friends and colleagues. Bill Soroka, six-time multi-bestselling author and mentor to thousands, whose friendship and wisdom have shaped my journey in ways I can never fully repay. Jen Neitzel, brilliant author of *On the Move: The Relationship-Driven 5 Point Marketing System for Mobile Business Success* and my trusted business partner at CNTDA—your energy and vision inspire me daily. Matt Miller, President of the California Independent League of Notaries (CLIN), whose leadership and advocacy elevate our entire profession. And Jennifer Cooper, Founder of the Central Valley Notary Network (CVNN), whose commitment to community has touched countless notaries. Each of you has encouraged me to share what I know and empowered me to help others serve with confidence and heart.

When I needed deeper insight into Remote Online Notarization in medical facilities, Selicia Young Jones and Amy Curtis generously shared their firsthand knowledge. Your expertise made this book more complete, and I'm truly grateful.

June Siegelhill, you gave your time, your keen eye, and your encouragement by pre-reading and editing this manuscript multiple times before final submission. Notaries do so much more than notarize, and you exemplify that truth. Thank you for caring about this project as much as I do.

My journey as an entrepreneur began with two extraordinary women who believed in me before I fully believed in myself. Sarah Stewart, who helped me start Lea's Place and taught me what it means to serve with compassion. And Joyce Gandelman, Esq., who guided me into mobile notary work and showed me that expertise and heart can coexist beautifully. Both of you gave me skills, confidence, and a lifetime of joy and purpose. I owe you everything.

I owe a tremendous debt of gratitude to the National Notary Association, which has been my professional home for over 20 years. As a member, California training instructor, and conference speaker, I've been given opportunities to grow, learn, and give back to this profession I love. Special recognition goes to Nicola Jackson, Director of Training and Education Services, whose consistent encouragement and unwavering support have meant the world to me. Thank you for believing in my voice.

And finally, to my dear friend Carol Ray, of blessed memory, you invited me into the original TNT weekly call (then known as the Breakfast Club) and changed the trajectory of my coaching career. Your generosity of spirit launched something I never imagined possible. I carry your memory with love and gratitude every single day.

ABOUT THE AUTHOR

Laura Biewer is a veteran notary, instructor, and advocate for professional excellence in specialty notary services. With over 20 years of experience and more than 35,000 notarizations performed, she has become a trusted leader in the notary community, especially in high-stakes environments like hospitals, hospices, and skilled nursing facilities.

As a sought-after educator and co-author of the Amazon best-selling book *Beyond Loan Signings*, Laura brings clarity and compassion to notaries, stepping into emotionally charged, time-sensitive situations. She has trained thousands of notaries across the country and is known for her practical wisdom, calm presence, and commitment to service.

Laura built a six-figure business through specialty work and intentional service, while continuing to teach, speak, and coach with passion. As she enters her "desirement" years, she remains focused on empowering notaries to show up confidently and competently where they're needed most.

Additional resources and to continue your learning visit **www.coachme-laura.com**

CONNECT WITH THE AUTHOR

Email: laura@coachmelaura.com

Free 15 min consult call: www.calendly.com/biewer

Follow Laura on Social Media:
- Facebook: facebook.com/GotNotary
- LinkedIn: linkedin.com/in/laurajbiewer
- Instagram: @lauraatyourservice

www.ingramcontent.com/pod-product-compliance
Lightning Source LLC
Chambersburg PA
CBHW060234030426
42335CB00014B/1446